BECOMING ALIEN

Reel Spirituality Monograph Series

The Reel Spirituality Monograph Series features a collection of theoretically precise yet readable essays on a diverse set of film-related topics, each of which makes a substantive contribution to the academic exploration of Theology and Film. The series consists of two kinds of works: 1) popular-level introductions to key concepts in and practical applications of the Theology and Film discipline, and 2) methodologically rigorous investigations of theologically significant films, filmmakers, film genres, and topics in cinema studies. The first kind of monograph seeks to introduce the world of Theology and Film to a wider audience. The second seeks to expand the academic resources available to scholars and students of Theology and Film. In both cases, these essays explore the various ways in which "the cinema" (broadly understood to include the variety of audio-visual storytelling forms that continues to evolve along with emerging digital technologies) contributes to the overall shape and trajectory of the contemporary cultural imagination. The larger aim of producing both scholarly and popular-level monographs is to generate a number of resources for enthusiasts, undergraduate and graduate students, and scholars. As such, the Reel Spirituality Monograph Series ultimately exists to encourage the enthusiast to become a more thoughtful student of the cinema and the scholar to become a more passionate viewer.

BECOMING ALIEN

The Beginning and End of Evil in Science Fiction's Most Idiosyncratic Film Franchise

SARAH WELCH-LARSON

CASCADE *Books* · Eugene, Oregon

BECOMING ALIEN

The Beginning and End of Evil in Science Fiction's Most Idiosyncratic Film Franchise

Copyright © 2021 Sarah Welch-Larson. All rights reserved.

Cascade Books
An Imprint of Wipf and Stock Publishers
199 W. 8th Ave., Suite 3
Eugene, OR 97401

www.wipfandstock.com

PAPERBACK ISBN: 978-1-7252-8300-8
HARDCOVER ISBN: 978-1-7252-8299-5
EBOOK ISBN: 978-1-7252-8301-5

Cataloguing-in-Publication data:

Names: Welch-Larson, Sarah, author.

Title: Becoming alien : the beginning and end of evil in science fiction's most idiosyncratic film franchise. / by Sarah Welch-Larson.

Description: Eugene, OR: Cascade Books, 2021 | Includes bibliographical references.

Identifiers: ISBN 978-1-7252-8300-8 (paperback) | ISBN 978-1-7252-8299-5 (hardcover) | ISBN 978-1-7252-8301-5 (ebook)

Subjects: LCSH: Science fiction films—History and criticism. | Alien films. | Good and evil in motion pictures.

Classification: PN1995.9.E93 W45 2020 (print) | PN1995.9.E93 (ebook)

Manufactured in the U.S.A.   DECEMBER 15, 2020

For Mom

TABLE OF CONTENTS

ACKNOWLEDGMENTS

Thank you to Elijah Davidson, who took my enthusiasm about religion and science fiction seriously, and to Dr. Kutter Calloway. Your encouragement, belief, and advice were invaluable throughout the process of writing this book.

Thank you to Chad Perman and the editorial staff at Bright Wall/Dark Room for being the first to publish me, and for pushing me to dig deeper and think harder about the things that seemed like minutae. Thank you to Josh Larsen at Think Christian for pushing me to write about faith without dancing around it.

My deepest thanks to my husband Josh, who introduced me to Dr. Catherine Keller's work, who encouraged me throughout the research and writing process, and who allowed Ripley and David and all the other characters in the *Alien* universe to take up residence in our home as temporary roommates. Thank you for arguing about the free will of robots with me.

INTRODUCTION

In the Beginning

S cience fiction provides a useful framework for considering issues from our own world in the context of another.[1] We can lift a concept—inequality, prejudice, gender,
fear of nuclear fallout, the value of a human life—and drop
it into a new and strange setting. This new environment,
like the light of an alien sun, illuminates the concept in a
way we cannot see on our own soil, trapped as we are in our
own contexts. In another world we can dissect it, feel it, pull
it apart and sew it together again. Here, in the real world, we
are blind, unable to express what we cannot see. There, in
the strange un-world of science fiction, the fog lifts. Even if
just for a little while, we can see our issues clearly, and their
borders, boundaries, definitions, and causes are thrown
into relief; perhaps we will find a space to understand them
a little better.

What better alien environment than the *Alien* films?

———

1. Suvin, *Metamorphoses of Science Fiction.*

Alien and its sequels have been picked over again and again in academic writing, ever since the first film was released forty years ago. *Alien* has been considered a problematic work because Ripley is reduced to her mother instinct,[2] and a great work because she channels that instinct into protecting the small and the weak.[3] *Alien* and its sequels have been considered as an anti-capitalist story,[4] a Vietnam War parable,[5] a refiguring of martyrs,[6] an eco-feminist satire,[7] a distillation of the fear of rape,[8] a tale about abortion,[9] a poorly-conceived explanation of creationism,[10] a haunted-house thrill ride,[11] a stalker film,[12] a triumph, a mistake.

Many of these readings are valid. Each of the *Alien* films takes the blueprint set for it by the original, and adapts the story to fit the intentions and interests of the people telling the story. The rousing action of *Aliens* inserts James Cameron's interest in megacorporations, machinery, and tough women into the series; the meditative introspection of *Alien3* strips away the machinery and adds a patina of David Fincher's trademark nihilism. *Alien: Resurrection* deals in Jean-Pierre Jeunet's exaggerated whimsy with a

---

2. Lev, "Whose Future?"

3. Gallardo and Smith, *Alien Woman.*

4. Byars et al, "Symposium on 'Alien.'"

5. Ward, *Aliens.*

6. Copier, "Maternal Martyrdom."

7. Janca-Aji, "Dark Dreamlife of Postmodern Theology."

8. McIntee, *Beautiful Monsters.*

9. Cobbs, "'Alien' as an Abortion Parable."

10. Johnson, "Prehistories of Posthumanism."

11. Ebert, *Sneak Previews.*

12. Zoller Seitz, "The original ALIEN was described by many critics, inaccurately, as haunted house movie in space, when it was actually a stalker film."

satirical bite. *Prometheus* and *Alien: Covenant* are more contemplative and digressive than the original spare *Alien*, which stands to reason: Ridley Scott was thirty-five years older when he made the prequels than he was when he directed the original. Each film also takes on a different meaning, depending on the person who watches it. Feminists read the film as feminist; Marxists read it as anti-capitalist. Like the alien the series is named for, each film adapts to its environment and its host.[13]

These isms are useful readings. They help us to tackle whatever problem we would like to face, allowing us to wrestle with one of the myriad issues of our world. But sexism, capitalism, and fear are not the core driver at the heart of the *Alien* story. They are facets, symptoms of a much deeper, more malevolent sickness. *Alien* could be a story symbolizing evil in specific situations: as a rape allegory, or a critique of colonialism. But like all great horror *Alien*, more accurately, is a meditation on the nature and existence of evil itself, in all its forms.

I have chosen to focus on the depiction of evil not just in the first *Alien* film, but also in its three sequels and two prequels.[14] Most readings of the world of *Alien* focus on one film in the series. This could be attributed to auteur theory: each film in the original quadrilogy was directed

13. Some writers refer to the alien as "the xenomorph," which is the name given to the species in *Aliens*. I have chosen to refer to the alien simply as "the alien," as it is the most consistently used name for the creature throughout the film series.

14. For simplicity's sake, we will leave texts like the *Alien vs. Predator* films, the *Alien: Isolation* videogame, and the myriad books, comic books, graphic novels, promotional shorts, and alternative scripts out of this discussion. These texts are interesting digressions and explorations of what could have been, but they remain extra-textual, apocryphal even: supplemental information at best and a distraction at worst. To understand the world of *Alien*, one needs only to understand the core six films; all other material is secondary.

by a different man. Each film, especially the first four, is tonally very different from its predecessors. *Alien* is cold and calculating, *Aliens* is rousing and exciting, *Alien3* is despairing and nihilistic, and *Alien: Resurrection* is irreverent and strange. If writing about the *Alien* films focuses on more than just one movie, the writing usually centers on the original four films, because these are united by the arc of Ellen Ripley's character. Writing about *Prometheus* usually compares the later film negatively to the original series, and typically gives precedence to the original *Alien*. Discussions of *Alien: Covenant* usually touch on *Alien* and *Prometheus* both, because these three were all directed by Ridley Scott.

I prefer a holistic approach, rather than a fragmented one. I find each of the six films in the *Alien* series to be vital, because each film expands on the concept of evil set forth by its predecessors, complicating that conception, and retroactively enriching readings of the films that came before. This recursive exploration of themes is innate to science fiction. In his book *Visions and Re-Visions: [Re]constructing Science Fiction*, Robert Philnus gets into the revisionist work of genre fiction, especially science fiction: "their common object . . . is instead concerned, not with what can be made from some publicly available text, but with what can be made of it, with its intrinsic of latent meaning—in which respect, the object of re-vision is hardly distinguishable from that of meaningful re-vision."[15] The most successful genre work does not merely repeat genre cliches. The best genre work operates within the constraints of its genre, while at the same time adding something new to that genre, redefining in some way what the genre is and can do in its respective context. This is particularly apparent in science fiction, which deals best in novel ideas

15. Philnus, *Visions and Re-Visions*, 298.

dropped into unfamiliar territories: time travel, artificial intelligence, alien life, all getting at new angles on the problem of what it means to be human. The *Alien* series is a microcosm of science fiction, with each subsequent film adding something new to the world presented in the last.

Alien is content to simply consider the existence of evil, and to sit in the shock that evil not only exists but is tangible. Evil in *Alien* is less a concept than a malevolent force.

Aliens lays out the practical results of the existence of evil, and posits that human beings have a fighting chance against it. The effect is a note of hope, both within the core of the story of *Aliens*, and added to the ending of the original *Alien*. We know at least that Ripley will survive the destruction of the *Nostromo*, and that alone gives credence to the hope coloring the end of the original film, hope that might have been too faint on a first viewing.

Alien3 confronts the reality that some evils are too difficult to defeat, let alone face. *Alien3* is notable because it is so introspective; the film marks the first time religion becomes an integral part of the script and plot, abandoning action for philosophy. *Alien3* sets a trend for the following films by resetting the ending of its predecessor, killing off Ripley's companions before the opening credits fade away and stranding Ripley by herself on a prison planet. *Alien* and *Aliens* both end in escape pods, while *Alien3* begins by crashing the escape pod, painting the previous films with a tone of fatalistic inevitability. The effect is a pendulum swing in the other direction, a hopelessness in the third film made more oppressive in comparison to the previous films. In comparison to *Alien3*, *Alien* and *Aliens* are both optimistic.

Alien: Resurrection returns to the religious themes of *Alien3*, but elects to push them past serious discussion into farce. It reverses Ripley's death at the end of *Alien3* by cloning her, handwaving away the end of the previous film, just as *Alien3* reversed the ending of its own predecessor. *Alien: Resurrection* grapples with evil, not as an outside force, but as something that is an intrinsic part of human beings: insidious, restless, and growing. *Alien: Resurrection* sets the stage for the prequel films by introducing for the first time in the series an android as a point-of-view character, and not as a piece of set dressing. Questions of the personhood of androids, which had been subtext in the previous three films, are made text in *Alien: Resurrection*. The farce of the plot underlines the film's very serious consideration of the sanctity of life, and of humanity's responsibility to break cycles of violence and exploitation.

Prometheus resets the series timeline, landing in the universe of *Alien*, but before the events of the first film. It is only tangentially interested in the alien creature itself, instead exploring the origins of alien—and human—life. *Prometheus* seizes upon *Alien: Resurrection*'s latent android theme; though the film ostensibly explores the origins of the alien creature, it is primarily interested in questions about free will and creation, especially about the creation of humankind, and in humankind's attempts to create AI "in our image."[16] If David, a "perfect" android created by humans, commits evil acts, did the evil come from him, or from the people who made him? *Prometheus* is trapped in a double bind: it is set in a universe familiar to moviegoers and horror fans, and it makes nods toward the alien first introduced in *Alien*, but it also seeks to blaze its own trail, leaving behind all preconceived notions about what makes an *Alien* movie an *Alien* movie.[17] It is a reboot, a reset, and a brand new story, simultaneously divorced from the

16. GEN 1:26 (NRSV).

17. Sobchack, "Between a Rock and a Hard Place," 33.

main themes of the rest of the *Alien* story and indebted to the groundwork laid by its predecessors. *Prometheus* complicates the story by making it nonlinear, ungrounded from time. Character motivations are conflated with broader concepts and mythology, and as a result, *Prometheus* comes across to most viewers as unlike an *Alien* movie, messy and flawed.

Alien: Covenant is a close sequel to *Prometheus*, and a necessary corrective; it clarifies the creationist themes of *Prometheus* while also bringing the series back firmly into the world of *Alien*. It also clarifies the character of the rogue android David, elucidating his motivations and painting his portrait in a more personal, more compelling, more tragic, and more terrifying fashion. Both prequels, as they consider the origins of humanity, dip into ideas about the source of evil: whether it is intrinsic to human nature, or some outside corrupting force. What had once been faint allusion to *Frankenstein* and *Paradise Lost* in *Prometheus* is made textual in *Alien: Covenant*. This allows the audience to stop straining to think about *why* the story progresses the way it does, and start considering how the story is going about itself.

Each film in the series builds upon the last, complicating and enriching the series' conception of evil as a whole. But what, exactly, *is* evil in the *Alien* films?

—

It can be tempting to claim that evil, at least in the *Alien* films, is mere nihilism personified by the alien. The alien appears to be an analogue for evil as Karl Barth described it—*das Nichtige*, "nothingness"—with the alien representing ravening, empty nothingness, a monster straight from the void. Barth's *das Nichtige* is the chaotic nothing in the void that postdates God, but tries to corrupt God's creation, always working in opposition to God. Like *das Nichtige*, the alien corrupts the human form, consuming it, hunting it, and using it as an incubator for its young, with no regard for the pain it causes, or even regard for questions about morality. Like the alien, *das Nichtige* is the space between the stars, the void, the emptiness that seeks to devour the good in the universe. Both the alien and *das Nichtige* come from nowhere, existing only to corrupt and to destroy. Even now, after forty years of *Alien* films, the audience cannot say with certainty where the alien comes from. If they have seen the prequels, the audience understands the events that lead to the creation of the alien, but the audience cannot explain exactly how the alien came to be, or where the building blocks of its being come from, or why those building blocks were created in the first place.

It is tempting to call the alien a slavering creature in the dark, the root of all evil, "nothing," and to claim victory over the text. But reading *Alien*'s horror tale through the lens of Barth's *das Nichtige* is too pat. It does discredit to both the theologian and the films; it is a misreading of both Barth and *Alien*. The alien as *das Nichtige* as evil in the *Alien* universe accounts only for the alien, but not for fallen human nature, nor for the evils committed by humanity, who as in real life commit evil in an all too logical fashion. It does not properly explain the issues of colonialism, sexism, exploitation, humanity's opposition to the Other, or humanity's opposition to itself. *Das Nichtige* is a good jumping-off point, a toehold on the edge of the alien abyss. But *das Nichtige* is an absolute, and the *Alien* films deal not in absolutes but in complexity.

Defining evil in the *Alien* films as violence is tempting, too. The alien exists to slaughter, and to slaughter horribly; it certainly poses an immediate physical threat to all who come in contact with it. But again, the alien is only part of the *Alien* films' depiction of evil, and the violence the alien enacts is not the only violence in the *Alien* universe. In *Alien*, violence must be enacted in order to protect humanity from the evil of the alien itself. Only violent actions can stop the alien from attacking; it lives to kill until it is itself killed. The *Alien* films have no room for pacifist responses to evil. Violence is both a destroyer of human life, and a valid method used to preserve it. Evil in the *Alien* films cannot be described simply as violence. Evil in *Alien* is more subtle, more complicated, and more insidious than mere violent action.

A still more complex reading of the *Alien* films would consider evil to be comparable to Kristeva's abject: that which "disturbs identity, system, order . . . [that which] does not respect borders, positions, rules."[18] The abject, like the alien, is repulsive, horrifying, sickening; it both intrigues and attracts the one affected, and it disgusts them, because it reminds them that there is something else out there that is distinctly not-them; it is Other. Abjection challenges the person experiencing it, because abjection invades the borders of what the experiencer considers to be good, upright, and normal. In her work *Powers of Horror* Kristeva outlines the importance of abjection in religion: concepts of what should be excluded from society because it defiles and pollutes the natural order of things are all shaped around what is abject. To sin, at least in part, is to embrace the abject.

The *Alien* films and the abject are no strangers: Barbara Creed's monstrous-feminine, which is built from Kristeva's conception of the abject, uses the original *Alien* as a cornerstone of its argument. In Creed's interpretation of Kristeva, the abject is both sickening and repellent, but also vital. It must "be tolerated for that which threatens

---

18. Kristeva, *Powers of Horror*, 4.

to destroy life also helps to define life."[19] Creed describes abjection as vital for horror movies. Horror, especially horror on the screen, is disgusting and sickening. Horror deals with borders and their invasion; the monstrous in horror film is a crossing of a border from the uncanny to our own world, with dire consequences. This invasion can be a border between societal norms and what is abnormal, or it can, as with body horror, be a border between Kristeva's "clean and proper body"[20] and distortions of the human form, which has lost its shape and integrity.[21]

Understanding evil in the *Alien* universe to be evil-as-abject, like evil-as-nothingness and evil-as-violence, is appealing. Certainly the abject helps shape our understanding of what is considered good and moral in both our world and these imagined worlds. But evil is not abjection, nor is the abject, strictly speaking, evil; abjection can reveal the borders of societal structures that have been created by evil intent, and can reveal structures that may have originated as neutral things, but have been exploited to bring about evil results.

The Company is, in some ways, the true villain of the original film.[22] The Company remains an important player in the sequels, but it is not a nameless, faceless entity. It is bureaucracy, colonialism, and capitalism, horrifically mundane in its selfish grubbing for a bottom line. The Company is not nothing: it is concrete, present, active. Nor is it, strictly speaking, violent, preferring to act via distant

19. Creed, *Monstrous-Feminine,* 9.

20. Kristeva, *Powers of Horror,* 102.

21. Creed, *Monstrous-Feminine,* 11.

22. Most viewers know the Company by the name Weyland-Yutani, but because that name does not exist in the first film, and because the Company takes several forms and names over the course of the series, for consistency's sake I will refer to it as "the Company."

orders and disinterested structure. When an executioner is needed, the Company falls back on their regulations and controls, or else calls in an outside actor, such as Ash in *Alien* and the Colonial Marines in *Aliens*.

The Company is evil, but it is not abject. It works by setting up red tape, directives, and protocols, all structures needed to run a megacorporation or a society. The Company is normal, usual, completely familiar to anyone who has needed to operate within ordinary societal structures. The Company cannot be abject. Instead, it sets the borders that the abjection of the alien tries to push through.

The protagonists of the *Alien* films (and the audience) treat the alien as abject, repulsive, and sometimes strangely beautiful.[23] But the alien is not the only example of abjection: because Ripley is a woman fighting the structures put in place by the Company, she is also herself monstrous-feminine—abject—and her abjection grows more and more obvious as the series goes on. The woman who defies the Company suits who doubt her story becomes a lone woman in a penal colony, and eventually becomes not a woman at all, but a clone, too close genetically to the alien to be considered human any longer: not a monster herself, but "the Grendel monster's mother."[24]

Evil in the *Alien* films is a both-and proposition, less binary than a spectrum. Evil in the *Alien* films can be concrete and conceptual, terrifying and mundane, malevolent and uncaring. The Company and the alien commit evil acts. So do the other humans, computers, and androids that populate the *Alien* universe. And in all the evil they do, they exploit.

Catherine Keller's *Face of the Deep: A Theology of Becoming* is an ideal interlocutor for the *Alien* films. Her

23. Kristeva, *Powers of Horror*, 11.

24. Jeunet, *Alien: Resurrection*.

work is a reclamation of the "deeps"[25] (in Hebrew, *tehom*) of the first two chapters of Genesis, a complication of traditional understandings of the universe and how it was created. Her complication is one that allows for possibilities rather than absolutes. Keller's work challenges traditional understandings of creation *ex nihilo*, arguing that the text of Genesis never says anything about God predating the chaos of the waters, in a reading that she admits "risks chaos"[26] but is far preferable to a colonial, patriarchal, simplistic interpretation that disregards the mystery of creation and provides a false foundation for our understanding of the universe and how it works.

For Keller, the chaotic deeps are not evil; they are simply what was there before all else. The *Alien* films establish themselves first as works set in the dark, blank cold of space. The *Nostromo* is just passing through, but space has always been there, and as far as we know, so has the alien. But although we read the void of space as inhospitable, we should not read it as evil. Space is a mirror for our fears and desires, containing both terrifying depths and sublime galaxies. "By itself the second verse of the Bible," says Keller, "however nonjudgmental toward the chaos, however free of any implication of evil and nothingness, can do little more than magnify—like a tiny well-ground lens—our fears and longings."[27] Space itself, in all its chaotic glory, forces us to consider that which is not-us, and be stunned by how small we are in comparison.

Keller challenges readings of evil as chaos and nothingness, especially Barth's *das Nichtige*. She claims the deeps "not as the evil, but as the active potentiality *for both good and evil*. So the capacity to resist any order, even a divine

25. Keller, *Face of the Deep*, xvi.

26. Keller, *Face of the Deep*, 5.

27. Keller, *Face of the Deep*, 25.

order, belongs to its indeterminacy."[28] She sees sin not as chaos, not as violence, but "as *discreation, that is, creaturely relations that deny and exploit their own interrelations*"[29] (emphasis hers). Evil is a denial of the inherent humanity and worth of the Other, a casual disregard of the value of life, a reduction of others from the status of *person* to the status of *tools*. In short, a distillation of the actions of both the Company and of the alien.

The *Alien* films, when viewed through the lens of Keller's work, are an exploration of evil-as-exploitation. This exploitation takes the form of violence, sometimes. But it can also take the form of careless treatment of others, as though they have no worth beyond being used as tools—a negation of their personhood. The alien exploits the human body, transforming it from independent, free relationship to unwilling incubator. The Company exploits its colonists and employees, sending them as expendable bait to catch the alien, which, in turn, the Company wants to use for its bio-weapons division. Evil in the *Alien* films is exploitation, the act of overstepping the freedoms of another.

The *Alien* films are not a manual on how to live, nor are they a morality tale. There are no pure characters in these films, only people, trying to survive, whether with good intentions or exploitative ones. It is important not to twist *Alien* to meet the understanding of morality, or, God forbid, the understanding of Scripture. Nor should Scripture be twisted to meet the alien. Both are important works, independent of each other, and each should not be exploited to provide an easy reading for the other. But *Alien* can be illuminated by a theological reading, and our understanding of our own conceptions of evil can be understood in dialogue with the *Alien* films. Keller's *Face*

28. Keller, *Face of the Deep*, 91.
29. Keller, *Face of the Deep*, 80.

of the Deep re-grounds our interpretation of the chaotic deeps at the beginning of time; her reading is also useful for re-centering readings of the *Alien* films that have grown skewed over time. Good science fiction does not preach. It provokes questions better than it answers them. The questions remain the same: they always boil down to "Who are we, and what are we to do?"

1

CREW EXPENDABLE

Alien

A lien opens in the dark: first blackness and a hint of stars, then a slow pan over a planet and its moons, title and credits sharp white against black, all outside light blotted out by the bulk of the planet. The title assembles itself patiently from a series of abstract lines, each letter spaced out from each other, making strange glyphs before resolving into a brief, familiar word: *Alien.*

In the beginning, there is a tower-like ship pushing its way insistently through the depths of the void. We start in medias res, although we do not know it yet. Soon enough, we will learn that the ship is not going away on a long voyage. The *Nostromo* is a commercial towing vehicle returning home, its refinery towers loaded with valuable ore. Its crew are not adventurers. They are truckers, shippers, ordinary blue-collar workers in the depths of space.

The audience is introduced to the interior of the *Nostromo* through a patient, roaming look through the ship's dark, empty corridors. The passageways are both massive and claustrophobic, octagonal, wider than a typical earthbound hallway, but crammed full of pipes, wiring, and switches: apparent chaos, but in a way that suggests some worker on board can make sense of the tangle, and that the tangle can make the ship go. As the camera floats through the corridors, we feel like invaders. There are no humans in sight, but evidence that they exist is everywhere: in the dippy birds on the kitchen table, in the wind chimes hanging in the doorway, in the papers rustling under an air duct outlet, and in the helmets staring blankly at computer screens on the bridge. For the first few minutes, we see no one, but we know people live here, somewhere in the innards of this massive cathedral-spired ship,[1] always already on their mission.

—

Catherine Keller's conception of the universe is nonlinear, unbounded by hard beginnings and endings; the universe exists in a constant state of becoming. The "In the beginning" of Genesis also begins in medias res,[2] the spirit of God hovering over the face of the deeps *("tehom")*, from which God creates the universe. These *tehomic* waters predate everything; they are a source of chaos, both frightening and full of delight, an unformed reality pregnant with unending, ever-changing possibilities, as deep as space, ebbing and flowing like the sea. They are both literal and figurative, the building blocks of the universe

1. The Nostromo was designed to look like a "cross between a tramp steamer and a cathedral" (Titan Books, *Alien: the Archive*, 32).

2. Keller, *Face of the Deep*, xvii.

scattered before their assembly into a recognizable shape. Keller marks the beginning not as a fixed point, but as "a beginning-in-process, an unoriginated and endless process of becoming"[3] that does not exclude any part of creation, but that seeks to enfold all parts of creation back into itself, iterating and re-iterating itself like a fractal.[4] Chaotic, dark deeps are no longer reduced to something to be feared—darkness is reclaimed as a good thing in a *tehomic* understanding of the universe[5]—but are understood to be rich with possibilities. The deeps are a source of *all* good, regardless of culture, creed, or communication.[6]

—

Like Keller's work to bring about a *tehomic* under-standing of the universe, *Alien* begins at the beginning, which is already in motion: the *Nostromo* is on a return voyage homeward, the Company's plot to capture an alien for their bioweapons division already in place. The whole of the film is set in the darkness of space, except when it is set in the darkness of a primordial planet, blurred by night-time and inhospitable weather, less a view of an alien world than a suggestion of one that might still be in the process of formation. The planet, like the *Nostromo*'s voyage and like creation itself, is in medias res.

The plot of *Alien* sets a template for all other *Alien* films to follow: under orders, a crew investigates something they should have left alone, and for their pains they are gruesomely eliminated by an alien monster, one by one. The crew of the *Nostromo* are ordinary people, despite their

3. Keller, *Face of the Deep*, xvii.

4. Keller, *Face of the Deep*, 44.

5. Keller, *Face of the Deep*, xvi.

6 Keller, *Face of the Deep*, xviii.

fantastic setting: they might sleep in flower-like cryopods while voyaging through the depths of space, but they wake up like anyone else, blinking slowly in the light, complaining that they are cold, sniping at each other over breakfast. There are only seven of them—five officers and two mechanics. Each one is a unique person, instantly recognizable in all their own quirks and neuroses. Their personalities bump off each other, harsh as the white clinical lights of the ship's interior, their breakfast conversation ebbing and flowing like chattering water.

The crew have been awakened halfway through their return trip with orders to find the source of an apparent SOS signal, unappealing work because it adds a detour to an already-long voyage. The Company they work for gives them no choice: the contract the crew is under stipulates that all shares they have already earned are forfeit if they do not obey orders. The audience instinctively understands the rules of the film's world because it maps so closely to our own. It is a world of contracts and pay bonuses, traffic control, bad working conditions, and worse company food. Orders from the Company become jobs, which lead to profits, which lead to extended contracts with the Company: a cycle of work that is bearable, not good.

None of the characters talk about their personal lives, nor about their plans when they reach Earth again, except to say that they want decent food once they are off the ship. For a film that has been interpreted to be about fear, about fear of rape, and about the knots human beings tie themselves into in order to fit into an economic system that is not built to favor them, *Alien* spends very little energy explicitly talking about those issues. It is an elegant example of the old adage about showing, not telling. None of the crew are in love, none are homesick, none have anyone waiting for them back home; or at least, if they do, they do not waste their breath pining about it.

———

The crew's understanding of *normal*, and by extension their values and actions, is dictated by protocol. Their adherence demonstrates the norms of their society, which maps closely to those of American society in the 1970s, with a key difference: there are women on board, with no one commenting about their gender or presence. Ripley and Lambert's positions as warrant officer and navigator are remarkable precisely because the film considers them to be unremarkable. The crew of the Nostromo was scripted to be gender-neutral, with freedom to cast male or female actors in any part[7]—the universality of *Alien*'s story is baked into its script. The other unremarkable aspects of life on the *Nostromo* reveal the crew's values and beliefs. Dallas (the captain) and Ash (the science officer) are the only two with access to Mother, the ship's computer, indicating a hierarchy; Mother is separated from the rest of the ship by a long corridor, a series of codes, and a door, with the computer itself housed inside a pristine white room lined with blinking lights, visually distinct from the crowded corridors of the rest of the ship. Mother's orders are relayed from the unseen Company, a further separation in the chain of command; this hierarchy is part of a larger system of rank and class that extends to everyone else on board. The officers—Dallas, Kane, Ripley, Lambert, and Ash—work on the upper deck, with the mechanics—Parker and Brett— sequestered below. The physical deck levels between ranks (and pay grades) provide a physical, ordered boundary, separating the crew from each other, exacerbating class

7. Rinzler, *Making of Alien*, 24.

differences between officer and mechanic. Parker and Brett poke at this boundary by dragging their feet during repair work and by attempting to achieve pay equity, a constant struggle that subsides only when the crew's physical well-being is threatened by an outside force. Each crew member has a slightly different definition of what is right, and what *should* be right; their collective moral compasses make up a microcosm of society. Although the crew's value systems diverge—Kane is adventurous, Lambert is cautious, and Parker and Brett are engaged in low-level class warfare with the others—the values they do share are built on a standard of normalcy that they never think about. The Company is in charge. There are procedures to maintain and protocols to follow. There is a job to do. The crew's lives are bounded by rules, both written and unspoken.

At the beginning of the film, the characters cannot see the boundaries that govern their lives, although Ash seems to be able to navigate them, and Dallas at least is aware that they exist; like any good ship captain he knows better than to steer too close to the edges. After Dallas and Ash break quarantine procedure by bringing Kane back on board, an alien organism attached to his face, Dallas defends his actions to Ripley, who is upset that protocol has been violated. "Protocol, my dear, is what they tell you to do," he snaps.[8] Dallas understands, even if only subconsciously, that the good of the crew is only in the Company's interests when that good serves that interest.

Ripley's adherence to protocol is grounded in a strong sense of what is right and what is typical. Before this voyage, procedure has never failed her; for Ripley, following protocol is beneficial because doing so will complete the job and result in bonus pay. Adherence means less friction, which means, perhaps, more contracts with the Company.

8. Scott, *Alien*.

Her actions are dictated by pragmatism and blind faith that Company protocols are good ones, specifically because she herself has never been harmed by these procedures; they create boundaries between what is safe and profitable and what is not. Boundaries are useful. They keep the airless void of space out of the *Nostromo*, and they provide a semblance of order in what would otherwise be a chaotic existence on board the ship: an imposed hierarchy, created by the Company, to keep the crew alive within the void of space and to help them to cooperate in achieving the Company's assignments. The crew accepts these boundaries as rules by which they are to live, neither good nor bad, but tolerable—the way the crew expects things to be, because they are just the way things are. When performing her duties, Ripley treats procedure as a good authority, but procedures can be twisted by those who know how to exploit them. The actions of the Company reveal their procedures not to be the only way for human beings to survive in space, but as a structure created by a corporation to exploit human beings.

—

The first sign that something has gone wrong is that the crew was awakened from hypersleep too early. They are ten months' travel away from home; the *Nostromo* has not reached the Outer Rim. They are deep in the borderless depths of space, ungrounded from any notions of normalcy except the ones they carry with them—Ripley's procedures and the orders from Mother to investigate the signal. Unspoken boundaries only become apparent when they are violated, and the crew's awakening and orders are unusual. They accepts their orders anyway. Their contract stipulates they stop to investigate signals that could be extraterrestrial life.

One deviation from the norm could be accepted as an anomaly; a string of deviations, as the *Nostromo's* mission becomes, is an aberration, an overturning of the crew's expectations about how things should go.

The crew's investigation is cursed from the start, with the *Nostromo* sustaining damage in what should be a routine landing—an apparent hull breach, a violation of the physical borders of the ship, trapping the crew on an inhospitable rock. The planet is "nearly primordial,"[9] according to Ash: no apparent indigenous life, no power, no footprints, nothing but bitter cold at night, a rocky landscape, and wind howling through an unbreathable atmosphere, a planet that is "formless and void."[10] And an apparent distress signal, the reason the crew was sent to investigate the planet: an opportunity for first contact or for rescue, perhaps, or a danger to the would-be rescue party. The signal beckons to the crew, enticing and frightening.

The crew's apprehension about finding the signal is a human one. The planet's desolate environment *feels* wrong, like some desaturated fantasy novel cover landscape, bleached of its color and sculpted from bones.[11] The source of the signal, too, feels wrong: when they first see it, the crew struggles to comprehend what it even is. It could be organic growth from the rocks around it, as far as they can tell. They ask each other repeatedly if the others are also "seeing this," as though the alien ship is a mass hallucination that will disappear if any of the crew name it for what it is. The derelict is massive, mind-boggling,

9. Scott, *Alien*.

10. Gen 1:2.

11. The planet's surface was indeed sculpted from bones and polystyrene (Rinzler, *Making of Alien*, 192).

frightening: its appearance defies the human definition of *spaceship*, and its sloping ribbed dark corridors and yawning orifices all scream *biological creation*. The ship looms over the landscape, its triple entrances black portals into nothingness: aberrations that recall female genitalia, their centers potential sources of terror, or of life. Their gaping holes recall Keller's reading of the nothingness at the beginning of the universe, with the *Nostromo*'s crew gaping back at the yawning abyss[12] of the derelict's entrances. Lambert is repelled, insisting repeatedly that they should "get the hell out of here."[13] Kane, by contrast, is enthralled, insisting that they "simply *must* go on."[14] He is eager to explore, enthralled by the unknown darkness before him, and by the possibilities that he will find something new and exciting within their depths—a Kellerian focus on origins and possibility, with no fear of the dark as a source of evil. His curiosity will lead him, Dallas, and Lambert to find the skeleton of some sad-eyed, elephant-like alien creature, much larger than any human, looking out of the cockpit of the derelict ship through something that could be a telescope, or could be a gun. The fossilized alien could be a part of the derelict ship, just as the derelict could be a part of the landscape surrounding it; the crew are in uncharted territory, with boundaries unmapped and unclear.

Dallas, Kane, and Lambert move on quickly, noting that the dead creature seems to have been fused into its seat, having become a part of the ship it once lived on. They also note that the creature's chest seems to have exploded from the inside, before moving on toward the ship's cargo hold. The camera, and by extension the audience, lingers on the creature's fossilized face for a moment longer; its mouth is

12. Keller, *Face of the Deep*, xv.

13. Scott, *Alien*.

14. Scott, *Alien*.

open in a scream, a harbinger of things to come. By being used as set dressing, the creature is reduced to the job it might have performed in life, molded into the chair it might have used to pilot the ship. In death, the creature is nothing more than a plot point, a grimacing specter in the dark foreshadowing the fate of the crew that discovered it long after its own death.

Kane's own fate is sealed when he is lowered into the derelict's cargo hold, his boots breaking through a layer of mist swirling above rows of leathery eggs. One of the eggs yawns open, and Kane, curious, peers inside to learn about its contents. A monster springs out, breaking through the thick glass in his EVA suit's visor, wrapping itself around his face and rendering him unconscious. Dallas and Lambert have to drag him back to the *Nostromo*.

The alien encounter is perplexing at first. The facehugger feeds Kane oxygen after knocking him out; it grips his face, but otherwise doesn't hurt him, unless it is itself disturbed. It bleeds acid when cut but otherwise does not fight back; eventually it drops off and dies, leaving Kane with memories of a bad dream about "smothering,"[15] but otherwise apparently unharmed. There seems to be no malevolent intent; perhaps this was all a misunderstanding, an animal reflex gone too far, an attempt on the part of the alien to communicate that ended badly. Ripley refers to the alien as "our guest"[16] when inquiring after Kane's well-being; the crew understands that the alien may very well be sentient, but that communication has broken down before it could ever be established.

Any illusions about Kane's well-being, and about any possible misunderstanding or communication with the alien, are shattered when the alien's young punches

15. Scott, *Alien*.
16. Scott, *Alien*.

its way through Kane's ribcage. Kane's demise is brief and sudden, first mistaken by his crewmates to be his choking on food, until his thrashing and cries of agony betray that this situation is far more serious. Kane's wails are difficult to hear, and worse to watch: he is in pain, and despite their best efforts, there is nothing the rest of the crew can do to help. When the alien bursts through Kane's chest, killing him, the crew can only stand and stare in mute shock: another instance of their gaping at an origin source.[17] Their shock extends for hours afterward. Dallas asks his subordinates if they have any words they want to say before they release Kane's body through the airlock; no one says anything, despite the fact that Kane seemed to be best liked among his crewmates. They commit his body to the void in stunned silence.

The alien negates Kane's humanity, first by literally covering his face, taking away both his consciousness and his agency, forcing him to be an unaware and therefore unwilling incubator for its offspring, a mobile cradle that must be eviscerated in order for the baby to be born. Kane's body is made into a creche, a transport, a first meal. He is turned into a tool for the alien, which has no remorse, no "delusions of morality," according to Ash.[18] The alien has no conception of sin. The crew's ideas about sin are less related to a religious framework than they are to the hierarchy instituted on board the *Nostromo*: Dallas has authority given to him by the Company, and the crew has protocols to follow in order to complete their mission. To violate protocol would be to disobey the Company, and by extension, to sin.

Keller, like Augustine before her, understands sin to be "not . . . disobedience but . . . *discreation, that is, creaturely*

17. Keller, *Face of the Deep*, xv.
18. Scott, *Alien*.

relations that deny and exploit their own interrelations"[19] (emphasis hers). This *discreation* is a return to the chaos of the world before God created it and gave it an orderly existence, a denial of the freedoms of human beings, who have been created from the chaotic depths and given a place within creational order. To exploit another is to dehumanize them, to state that they have worth only as tools or toys, and not as created beings with the spark of divine life. The crew of the *Nostromo* are exploited at every turn, including by the alien.

The alien itself is abjection made incarnate throughout its lifecycle, less an independent creature than a monster designed to exploit the human body in order to propagate its own species.[20] In the egg it flutters, fishlike, behind a pulsing membrane inside a suggestive orifice: an image of motherhood distorted into something monstrous.[21] As the facehugger parasite, it appears to have skeletal human-like hands with joints and nails for grasping, a segmented tail, a pair of lungs, all covered with a skin that looks horribly like human flesh—more distortion that blurs the line between human being and inhuman monster. The hands grasp the alien's victim by the face, allowing the creature to deposit its offspring down the victim's throat, transforming the human being into an incubator for its young. The chestburster version maintains the same sickly color as the facehugger, this time bullet-headed, beginning its stage of the alien life cycle before chewing its way out, punching through its host's ribs and killing them in the process of delivery. It is spotted with human blood and gore, sporting a tiny jaw full

19. Keller, *Face of the Deep*, 80.

20. An early script reveals that the alien was bred to be a bioweapon by the Company, and that the crew of the Nostromo are intended to be the alien's "guinea pigs." Rinzler, *Making of Alien*, 66.

21. Creed, *Monstrous-Feminine*, 17.

of sharp, metallic teeth, and has no eyes to speak of. The fully grown alien, finally, is both masculine and feminine in form, a genderless neither-nor. It is an *it* that might be intelligent, or might just be a hungry animal, dripping in slime and malice, as eyeless as its chestburster incarnation. It has a double jaw and a shining black carapace, with biomechanoid pipes and wires covering its muscles, allowing it to blend in with the pipes and tubing lining the corridors of the *Nostromo*. Each version of the alien has acid for blood and a drive to kill everything in its path. It is unclear if the alien is aware of the pain and terror it causes as it impregnates and kills Kane, then stalks and picks off the rest of the crew, one by one. It is unclear why the alien kills, and kills again: the crew never sees it eating, and it takes no trophies.[22] We never learn if the alien is sentient, if it understands what it is doing, or if it is merely following an urge to hunt, a much larger predator than the ship's own cat. Whatever the reason may be, the alien exploits the crew. Its intentions and purposes—whether a biological drive, or a malevolent need to harm—do not matter. The effect of dehumanization is the same regardless.

The alien is the most obvious example of discreation in the film, literally dismembering its hosts, but the crew is dehumanized by another actor throughout the course of the film, one we as an audience never see. The Company sent the crew to investigate the derelict ship's distress signal—the apparent SOS that turned out to be a warning— on purpose. The Company knew of the existence of the alien already (exactly how is left unexplained) and they

22. In a deleted scene, Ripley finds Dallas in a side corridor. In this version of the film Dallas was not killed in the airlocks, but taken by the alien and turned into a cocoon, soon to become an egg himself, the boundary between human and alien blurred further than the alien's humanoid shape could ever do (Scott, *Alien*).

want it for their bio-weapons division. "All other priorities rescinded," Ash's orders from the Science Division read. "Crew expendable."[23] The safety of the crew of the *Nostromo*, as well as their bodies and their physical and mental well-being, are forfeit, the boundaries between their bodies and the outside, and between their existence as humans and as tools, rendered suddenly porous. The alien comes snarling out of the dark to tear down those boundaries and force the crew to understand that the water they swim in is not water; it is a hostile environment, and might as well be molecular acid. The crew are no longer a crew, but bait, transport, and tools, all meant to retrieve a ravenous monster so that the monster itself can be pulled apart, tested, and turned into a weapon. The alien may dehumanize the crew, but the Company attempts to exploit every living creature it comes into contact with, worth only the profits they can provide. Keller posits that sin-as-discreation is habitual, a cycle of denial and repetition that solidifies over the years into societal norms, eventually becoming value systems in which some human beings are more highly valued than others: sexism, racism, inequitable economic systems, and so on. These habits are made by unconscious choice: the decision to go along with the unbalanced system, regardless of the harm it might do to another, all because the choice is made easiest for the person doing the choosing, until conscious decisions are obscured and the choice to sin becomes a choice to go along with the flow of an established path.[24] To the Company, the crew is as significant as the lines of code that spell out their names, and nothing more; they are not people, but the ideas of people, things flying in the dark at the mercy of a ravening monster and an uncaring android. When Ripley discovers the Company's orders, and

23. Scott, *Alien*.
24. Keller, *Face of the Deep*, 80.

Ash's part in carrying them out, she storms through the *Nostromo*, calling Ash's name in an attempt to engage with him on a personal level. In response, Ash assaults her, first physically, then sexually, denying her agency by knocking her unconscious, then denying her personhood by violating her autonomy. His assault reveals the Company's view of the entire crew. Their constructed boundaries and their lives are violated, and they are reduced from *you* to *it*.

The crew are not innocent of dehumanization, either. The moment they learn that Ash is a robot (and an agent of the Company), the crew abandons any ideas they might have had about his agency and personhood. Parker exclaims, "It's a robot! Ash is a goddamn robot!"[25] *He* is reduced to *it*: an object, a tool at the mercy of the company, but this one sentient and fully aware and accepting of its function. Things beget things, careless use begets use, and evil begets evil. Ash, who exists first as a cipher and an outsider, then as a thing and a nonhuman object, has a twisted sense of morality. He is an object, who treats his fellow crewmembers as objects to be manipulated, because he sees the rules and norms of the Company he works for, and understands those rules for what they are: instructions meant to keep the crew pacified, unaware of how little control they have in their situation, and unaware of the Company's intentions toward them. The protocols in place are written with the apparent intent to preserve human life, so the crew does not question the Company's commitment to treat them as human until it is too late.

———

By the time the crew realizes what the Company has done to them, half of them are dead: Kane eviscerated, Brett

25. Scott, *Alien.*

and Dallas taken by the alien, Ash reduced to the wires and beads that make up his insides. Besides a brief exchange between Ripley and Ash, in which Ripley attempts to understand the crew's chances of survival and in which Ash reveals his admiration for the alien purely because it is inhuman, the crew are all alone. They have no support from the Company, which signed their death warrants by sending them to find the alien in the first place. They have no room to debate their place in the Company, if they still work for the Company at all. They only have time to act, to cut their losses and run. If the alien catches up with them, they will die. Critical thought about their position can come later.

They take action, abandoning all other priorities. Rather than being paralyzed by the realization that they are tools, they exercise agency, choosing to activate the self-destruct and to take their chances in the shuttle. They might be trapped beyond the Outer Rim, but floating in a lifeboat beyond human outposts is preferable to never making it back alive to the rest of humanity. The possibility of survival and life dwells on equal footing with the possibility of death in the unknown wilds of space, or, as Keller would call them, the deeps.[26]

Ripley's decision to act is most striking, because up until this point she has been a company woman through and through. She had insisted on proper quarantine procedure; she oversaw the repairs done by Parker and Brett; she pushed back against Ash's decisions, questioning the apparent aberration that was the Science Division taking over the mission of the *Nostromo*. Ripley is uncomfortable belowdecks; she is comfortable performing the duties required by someone of her rank, including taking over command when protocol demands it. She hardly hesitates when refusing Dallas's orders to break quarantine procedure.

26. Keller, *Face of the Deep*, 21.

Even after Ash tells her, Parker, and Lambert that they have little chance of survival, Ripley follows procedure to the letter: she refuses to follow along with Lambert's plan to use the ship's self-destruct until the crew is small enough to fit inside the shuttle, choosing instead to appeal to the higher authority of the ship's computer. But once she learns that the ship's computer—and Ash—are co-conspirators with the Company to use the crew as bait to obtain the alien, Ripley agrees to destroy the *Nostromo*; she herself is the one who sets the self-destruct.

Even the self-destruct betrays the Company's attitude toward its employees. Perhaps the mechanism was developed to keep the crew from tripping it accidentally, and therefore losing both crew and expensive payload, but the steps needed to activate the self-destruct are slow, ponderous, and difficult: heavy two-handed switches and delicate screws are not conducive to emergency situations. By tripping the self-destruct, Ripley discovers one more way that she is at the mercy of a company that will force her to contort herself into various painful positions in order to squeeze further profits out of her labor, and which will not blink when she cannot perform the tasks required of her. They will extend her no sympathy, but will allow her to be destroyed by their own equipment as she attempts, alone and afraid, to complete her job.

—

Despite its cold efficiency, the film does not share the values of the Company whose orders doom the crew to death and dismemberment by a malevolent force. Director Ridley Scott takes care to humanize every single member of the crew. They may not have much by way of backstory—backstory is not important when you are running for your life—but they each have a name, a personality, a unique reaction to the monster in their midst. When Brett wanders off to find the ship's cat, the camera treats him as an equal, following him because his point of view is important. Brett has been the butt of jokes up until this point, treated as though he is dim by the rest of the crew. Alongside the rest of the crew, Brett is a pawn in the interpersonal politics of the ship. Alone, he is a person, allowed to walk through the cargo bay upright and with dignity. He can tilt his face toward the water droplets falling from the ceiling, letting the rain hit his cap and fall into his mouth, revealing a deeper inner life than his limited vocabulary previously indicated. He can pause and take a moment for himself, no longer playing Parker's echo, at least until the fully-grown alien reveals itself for the first time in front of him. Brett's death is made more upsetting, and more tragic, because he dies not as a one-note character, nor as a tool, nor a job title, but as a person.

As with people, so with other life: the film treats it all, except the alien, as valuable and worth preserving. As Ripley preps the shuttle for takeoff, she hears the ship's cat—Jonesy—meowing over the radio. Procedure might dictate that the remainder of the crew abandon the cat with the ship; a coldly pragmatic person might even go so far as to hope that the cat could distract the alien long enough to keep it occupied while the crew made their escape. Compassion has other dictates. The cat might not be human, but it is still a sentient creature. Ripley goes after Jonesy without hesitation, rather than abandoning him to the alien and the ship's self-destruct. There is inherent worth in life, regardless of location. Whether within the confines of a constricting social hierarchy or lost in the unstructured chaos of outer space, life deserves to be allowed to live.

———

Ripley's decision to adhere to a strict moral code, to fight the alien, to detonate the expensive payload in order to save the remainder of the crew, and to go back and rescue the ship's cat all trace her development into someone who is fully conscious of the existence of the evil that lurks within the Company's systems of power. She still depends on their equipment for survival, but by the end of the film, she has rejected the ethos of the Company—working to destroy the alien against the Company's direct orders, trying to save the remainder of the crew regardless of their class status, destroying the payload and ship's profit in the hopes that doing so will save human lives. *Alien* marks Ripley's awakening through her conscious decisions to no longer adhere to the Company's values nor participate in their protocols. She breaks away from cycles of disrelation, and in so doing, both takes responsibility for her own actions within an inequitable system and reaffirms the value of human life.

2

AN EXPRESS ELEVATOR TO HELL

Aliens

A*lien* is small, as self-contained as the ship the film is set in. It depicts, simply, the exploitation of one small crew by one heartless Company order, one undercover android, and one unwelcome passenger—high stakes at relatively small scale. True to its title, *Aliens* gives the audience more: more aliens, as well as more characters, with more capacity for greater evil. *Aliens* raises the stakes by compounding the scale of the story being told: instead of a single ship and a crew, the setting and cast are a planet and a colony. *Alien* revealed that evil is not just an abstract possibility; it is real and tangible as well as existential. *Aliens* fleshes out the world of its predecessor, imagining what the realities of living under an exploitative company would be like. Where *Alien* was concerned with the horror of discovering the existence of evil, *Aliens* is concerned with the action that is necessitated by this discovery, and the reality that asserting control over chaos is impossible.

—

Aliens takes the raw-boned universe of *Alien* and adds meat to its skeleton. The audience watching *Alien* understands that the *Nostromo* is a microcosm, a snapshot of a much larger universe with all the bureaucrats, red tape, class tension, and societal structure that a disagreement during breakfast over a simple pay bonus can imply. The story told in *Alien* raises more questions than answers:

- Where did the alien come from? Are there more of them out there?

- What will happen to Ripley, now that she is the last survivor? Will there be any repercussions for the destruction of the alien or the deaths of the crew of the *Nostromo*?

- What kind of a company would knowingly send a crew of seven to their deaths?

- What kind of a universe is this, that such a company appears to be profitable? Is the Company an aberration, or do people disappear all the time without anyone questioning their absence?

James Cameron, who picked up the threads of the story that Ridley Scott left behind, chose not to answer all of these questions. Cameron's version of the story is forward-looking, not interested in origins or *whys*, only in *what nexts*. Questions of the existence and origins of other life in the universe are left behind, and so remain a mystery.[1]

[handwritten margin note: Separates him from modern franchise hacks]

1. The film hints that there is other life known in the universe, but humans appear to be the top of the food chain. The Colonial Marines banter about sexual encounters with Arcturians, apparently an alien

The audience—and the characters in the story—learn nothing more about the origins of the alien. Any questions about the skeleton in the derelict ship from the first film are abandoned; any ideas about the intricacies of a possible alien society are left by the wayside. The audience knows there are more aliens in the universe, thanks to the film's plural title: the question about the existence of other life in the universe is answered before the film has even begun.

The rest of Cameron's answers are logical extensions of the world of *Alien*. A company that would carelessly send seven of their employees to investigate a malevolent life form with the intent of monetizing that life form would do so again without thinking twice. Such a company would care only about profits and outcomes, unconcerned with the human cost so long as their ledgers remain in the black.

Aliens expands the world of *Alien*, leaving the stifling world of the *Nostromo* behind, but not abandoning it entirely. The sequel presents variations on the themes first apparent in the original, similar and yet different: branches from a fractal that spiral out and inspire questions of their own.

———

The film opens much like its predecessor, with a slow pan over deep space to a small ship, drifting its way between the stars. This time, the ship has a familiar shape. No towering refinery spires, just an escape shuttle—the very same one from the end of *Alien*. Every surface inside the ship is covered with glittering dust. The lighting is no longer

———

species that is never mentioned again. The Marine drop ship bears a logo titled "Bug Stompers," with the motto "We Endanger Species" emblazoned below a war eagle wearing a massive pair of sneakers, its wings tucked in an attack dive (Cameron, *Aliens*).

the yellowy gray of *Alien*'s color palette, but a dark blue, cold and deep. The shuttle has been drifting for a long time. When a deep-space salvage team carves its way through the door, they do so with a laser at the end of a block-shaped robot arm, blunt-edged and menacing.

The crew find Ripley sleeping in the shuttle, and bemoan their lost salvage (and lost pay). The universe kept spinning while Ripley was asleep. Her rescue took sixty years, instead of the expected six weeks. In the intervening decades she herself lost everything: ship, crew, the life she once had, the family she left back home, her career, her peace of mind, her credibility. She may have outwitted the alien sixty years before, but she cannot outrun the consequences. While she recovers in the hospital, and even after, she endures nightmares about the alien that decimated the crew of the *Nostromo*. In all her dreams she too is made a victim, with the alien head rearing impossibly high beneath the skin of her stomach. Every night she wakes up screaming, covered in sweat, massaging her chest, as though the dream-alien has just broken through her own flesh.

The scenes after Ripley's rescue are lit cold and white, clinical and sterile; she might be back among other human beings, but she is just as isolated as she had been when she was asleep on the shuttle, haunted by bad memories and by the Company's disinterested disbelief in her report of the alien and the destruction of the *Nostromo*. Later, when the film becomes a rescue mission, and then a war movie, its aesthetics will take on a muddy flavor, colored by Ripley's PTSD and the braggadocio of a squad of Colonial Marines, heavily armed and eager for a fight.

Like *Alien*, *Aliens* is about a crew investigating a possible encounter with extraterrestrial life, and finding a situation they are unprepared for. Unlike *Alien*, the characters in *Aliens* go into their investigation clear-eyed, aware of the existence of alien life; the investigators are not civilian space truckers diverted from their ordinary shipping schedule, but a squad of soldiers already experienced with close encounters; the team is rounded out by an android and a Company man, with Ripley as their consultant. The planetoid where Ripley's crew found the first alien is now a colony, populated by Company employees; when the Company loses touch with their colony, they call in the Marines to exterminate a possible alien invasion.

Aliens is consumed by war.[2] When Ripley joins the Marines on their mission to the colony, she trades the pale palette of the hospital for an environment that is dark blue and green in hue, the surfaces stained like fatigues. The score is laced with the staccato of a snare drum performing a parade march. James Cameron's boxy machinery, heavy and militant, permeates the aesthetic of the film. The camera glides across the muscles and guns of the Marine characters, setting them up to be, as their sergeant declares, "absolute badasses."[3] These characters (men and women both, as the Nostromo's ungendered division of labor extends to the armed forces, still a novelty in the 1980s) are people of action, spoiling for action. Their own actions will spiral out into myriad unintended consequences, which will demand further decisive action in return, a feedback loop of action and uncertainty. To freeze, according to *Aliens*, will be to stagnate, to become trapped. Some of them will be trapped by others' inaction, through no fault of their own. Most of them will die.

———

2. The tagline on the film's poster makes this explicit, stating, "This time it's war."

3. Cameron, *Aliens*.

Keller's *tehomic* view of the world makes space for action and reaction amidst uncertainty. The deeps of Genesis are chaotic, troubling in their multiplicity and unknowability. In response to this uncertainty, says Keller, western thought is colonial, bent on domination over the unknowable. "The abiding western dominology can with religious sanction identify anything dark, profound, or fluid with a revolting chaos, an evil to be mastered, a nothing to be ignored,"[4] she says, and in so describing colonialist thought patterns, she also describes the Company's attempts to control its world.

The Company is not just a shipping business, but a megaconglomerate working to develop settlements on other worlds, terraforming entire planets. Such a company can treat people as expendable, and get away with it. In *Aliens*, the Company is given a name: Weyland-Yutani.[5] The name implies mergers of large corporations into larger ones, a practice of bureaucracy and hostile takeovers. From offhand mentions of bio-weapons divisions and terraforming in the dialogue, the Company is a super-conglomerate, big enough to have a fleet of expensive commercial towing vehicles like the Nostromo, as well as docks, loading bays, terraforming colonies, investors, insurance specialists, board members, and red tape. Their motto is "Building Better Worlds," and their business appears to be everything, including terraforming.[6] They manufacture massive air-processing units meant to turn out worlds that are close

4. Keller, *Face of the Deep*, 6.

5. In *Alien*, the beer can props and computers on board the *Nostromo* had been labeled "Weylan Yutani" [*sic*], but *Aliens* is the first film in the series to make the company name explicit (Cameron, *Aliens*).

6. Their logo is on the air processing unit used to terraform planets, on the files in Ripley's inquest, and, in a deleted scene, on the big wheel trike a child rides through the terraforming colony (Cameron, *Aliens*).

enough to Earth's atmosphere to be considered habitable, employing families of colonists to do the terraforming work for them. The planet the *Nostromo* once landed on is now one such colony. It even has its own name: LV–426, more catalog code than title. The Company's methods are cold and efficient, with no room for romanticism. Even their planet names are rooted in efficient character strings, with no names based in literature or in honor of scientific heroes. If anything were to happen to the colony's residents, the Company could easily wipe the slate, throwing away the remains of their old colony just as easily as they throw aside Ripley herself.

The work of the Company is calculated to control situations, to control outcomes, and to control profits, an ethic that is at direct odds with Keller's *tehomic* view of the world. For Keller, "*tehomic* theology does not worship chaos . . . the flowing potentiality of each actuality, each creature, realizes itself in limitation." The deeps are most profound when they come into contact with creation, unbounded possibility contrasted with concrete modes of being, complex creation emerging from and in contrast to chaos.[7] By terraforming entire planets, by covering up the destruction of the *Nostromo*, and by trying to obtain an alien for its bioweapons division, the Company attempts to control that chaos, denying the possibility that anything outside their power has the ability to become, to grow, to flourish. They work to stamp out all other life besides their own.

——

Upon Ripley's rescue and recovery, the Company holds an inquest to understand the events that led to the

7. Keller, *Face of the Deep*, 7.

loss of the *Nostromo* and its crew. The loss would have been a cold case before Ripley's reappearance: most of the suits interviewing Ripley are too young to have been born before the events of *Alien*. The *Nostromo* would have been given up for lost decades ago, but now, with Ripley alive and before them, the Company has someone to blame for the loss of millions of dollars' worth of equipment. Throughout the inquest, a screen behind Ripley flicks through pictures of the crew, but Ripley is the only person in the room to mention her crewmates, let alone call them by name. The suits are much more interested in what happened to their property than what happened to the crew who tended it. Machinery is rendered more valuable than human beings.

Ripley repeats herself over and over again until she loses her patience. "How many different ways do you want me to tell the same story?" she snaps at the chain-smoking Company bureaucrats.[8] But she is invested in her tale, despite the fact that she wants no part in it; she will not back down from the truth, for fear that there are more of the same aliens out there in space, that others will suffer the same fate as the crew of the *Nostromo*. Most of all, she is afraid that the Company will try again to bring an alien back for study, as they had ordered the *Nostromo* to do. "If one of those things gets down here, that *will* be all!" she shouts at the board members who dismiss her story, "You can kiss all of that goodbye!"[9] Ripley's concern, as it had been when she first refused Dallas's order to break quarantine, is for the safety and well-being of others, whom she fears will be overrun by the uncaring bureaucratic machinery of the Company.

Her concern comes to nothing. Perhaps the Company is genuinely attempting to understand an incident for which

8. Cameron, *Aliens*.

9. Cameron, *Aliens*.

they have no record, in their own bureaucratic way; perhaps it is a cover-up for a larger Company conspiracy to hide their intentions to obtain an alien for research. Whatever the case, Ripley is the perfect scapegoat, a difficult woman who dropped out of the void with a story she herself admits is hard to believe. Perhaps her outburst was the opening they needed to justify their actions, but the board suspends her license indefinitely, and subjects her to probation and ongoing psychiatric evaluation. Their decision is final and inevitable. What chance could one individual have against such an impersonal, all-controlling structure?

The inquest is closed; the board members brush past her after she is stripped of her flight officer status. Ripley is forced to work as a loader in the docks—grunt work—because the hard labor is the only job she can get. When one of the suits remarks that "it's great that she's keeping busy,"[10] the comment is a backhanded slap in the face, a reminder that she has been stripped of her class, her livelihood, and her credibility, all through no fault of her own, at the whim of a company she once poured her soul into but who never regarded her as anything more than a face and a name and a piece of bait for a monster they valued more highly than human lives. In *Alien*, Ash told Ripley he admired the monster because it had no "delusions of morality."[11] In *Aliens*, the source of Ash's admiration is made clear: he was created and directed by a company that shared the alien's disregard for the value of human life. Ripley loses her privacy along with her rank: the company man casually mentions that he has read her file. He lists her nightmares and her PTSD symptoms in front of another person as though he is remarking on her new haircut, and not on the trauma Ripley has endured in service of the

10. Cameron, *Aliens*.
11. Scott, *Alien*.

company that forced her to undergo the trauma in the first place, then threw her aside when the repercussions became too complicated for them to handle.

———

Only after the inquest does Ripley learn that the planet is inhabited by sixty or seventy families in the Company's employ. These families are terraforming colonists, working to transform entire planets into habitable spaces for other human beings. Terraforming is a natural fit for colonialist ideals. Like terraforming, colonialism is an attempt to bring the colonized under control by forcing it to change to suit the needs of the colonizer: an attempt to negate the personhood of the colonized, to impose order on a perceived chaos: "building better worlds,"[12] according to the Company's own motto. The colonists embody the work of colonialism, changing the atmospheric makeup of LV-426 to fit the lungs of the human beings walking the planet's surface.

The colonists' use of terraforming to change LV-426 to suit their needs is a natural extension of the Company's ethic of control, and of their cavalier use of people as tools: families are sent out as exploratory feelers, searching for resources the Company could add to their portfolio.[13] The Company is not in the business of interstellar humanitarian work. The "better worlds" they build come not from charitable desires but from intent to increase Company profit. By cooperating with the Company's business goals,

12. Cameron, *Aliens.*

13. The colonists' terraforming of LV-426 recalls the alien egg room within the derelict ship in *Alien,* which creates its own atmosphere, and the Engineer stockpile in *Prometheus,* which generates air that is clean enough for human beings to breathe.

colonists may be paid, or fed, or given the means to start families, but they also further the goals of the Company. The path of least resistance—working for the Company without questioning its motives—is the path of no resistance at all. The Company's motives are underlined by profit, with people serving as tools to further that profit. All personhood is negated by bottom lines.

After the inquest, the Company sends the colonists a directive to go find Ripley's derelict ship, and by extension her alien. Shortly afterward, the Company loses all contact with the colony, prompting them to send the Colonial Marines out to investigate. By the time the Marines arrive, the colonists are gone, leaving behind acid-eaten floors and torn wiring spilling out from the walls, victims of an apparent alien encounter. The Marines find only chaos in the remains of the colony: a bar door flapping in the wind, holes in the ceiling, rain pouring through into half-empty coffee cups and soaking into abandoned food: snapshots of small lives sacrificed by the Company in the hope of obtaining new and more profitable technology. The Marines investigating the colonists' disappearance will disappear themselves, another consequence of the Company's attempts to control LV–426 and its inhabitants, another series of lives permanently erased, each one with their own consequences to follow.

—

Lieutenant Commander Gorman is the ostensible leader of the Marines. He is inexperienced, having only completed one live combat drop before the mission to LV–426. He is also incompetent, incapable of remembering the names of his own squad members correctly, and unable to operate except by script. Instead of earning the respect of his subordinates, Gorman tries to demand it by asserting control over things he can never control, acting as though he is in command of the situation on LV–426 rather than being in command only of a squad of people sent to assess the situation. The Marines know of his inexperience, and they resent him for it. In turn, Gorman fails to rise to the occasion, sending them into a nuclear terraforming plant armed with armor-piercing rounds. Ripley has to remind him that doing so has endangered the lives of everyone in the colony: one misfired bullet could set off an explosion that would kill everyone around them for miles. When reminded of his mistake, Gorman orders the Marines under him to unload their weapons without telling them why. Resentful and untrusting, the squad holds back their ammunition. They fire on a nest of aliens on first sight, and in the fracas, their firepower damages the plant, while the aliens decimate the squad—more acts of discreation, facilitated by structures of domination and mistrust. As his men are slaughtered, Gorman loses control over himself, freezing up, until Ripley takes over the controls of the ATV and drives the few survivors free of danger.

One of those survivors, Corporal Hicks, is quiet, calm, and collected, even in combat. He stands as a foil for both Ripley and Gorman. Gorman outranks Hicks, but Hicks commands the respect of his squadmates without having to demand it or ask for it. He is a man of action with a quiet voice, uninterested in trying to control the chaos that erupts around him, only in trying to understand it well enough to survive. Like the other Marines in his outfit, Hicks paints his body armor. Unlike the others, his decorations are not braggadocio (*"El Riesgo Siempre Vive"* on a chestplate, *"Adios"* on a gun, *"I Fly the Friendly Skies"* on a pilot's helmet).[14] Instead, he has a small red heart

14. Cameron, *Aliens*.

painted on his chest, covered by a small padlock; the only other decoration is a phrase circling around a bullet hole in the armor for his upper arm, which states simply, "Born Again." Hicks is keenly aware of his own mortality, and he knows his limitations: he will die someday, and he is lucky to be alive today. His understated body armor matches his attitude: he keeps calm in action, telling his few remaining comrades to "stay frosty"[15] in order to survive the night. When Ripley breaks the soldiers out of the alien nest in the ATV, her action saves their lives, but it also blows the transmission on the vehicle, rendering it useless. Hicks maintains his cool head, despite the unexpected chaos they have all escaped, forcing Ripley to ease down. Hicks's collected demeanor allows the few remaining survivors to stop and regroup, to take stock of their situation before planning their next move, trapped in the confines of their makeshift base in colony headquarters, alone and without hope of rescue on the edge of chaos.

—

The chaotic wilds of LV–426 are not bad. Nor is society; they are merely environments and systems in which people live and work and breathe. But the chaos of the planetoid drives the fragile nature of human existence into stark relief, exposing the weaknesses of the Marines' chain of command. The rescue party find themselves in uncharted territory, separated from the noise of more settled parts of space, and the result is that the Company's attempts to control chaos are laid bare. The Company wants to tame the planet through terraforming, and it wants to obtain the alien. The planet itself is not bad; it is a source of possibility. It brings Ripley into contact with the alien, but it also brings

15. Cameron, *Aliens.*

her into contact with Newt, an eleven-year-old girl and the lone survivor of the alien attack on the colony. As with Jones in *Alien*, so with Newt in *Aliens*: Ripley's instinct is to befriend and protect a being who is smaller and more helpless than she is.[16] Ripley shows the traumatized girl patience and understanding when the Marines give her up as broken. Gorman thinks of Newt as braindead, unable to respond to his questioning, but Ripley understands the horrors Newt has endured more than anyone else. She coaxes the girl out of her shell, promising that she will not leave Newt behind, without a thought for her own survival.

—

Ripley's protective instinct is not extended to the lone non-human member of the rescue party. She reacts violently when she learns that Bishop, an apparent civilian accompanying the team, is an android. Her reaction is somewhat understandable—the last Company android she dealt with tried to kill her—but the degree of her distrust boils over to hatred. Even after Bishop extends sympathy to her over Ash's betrayal, Ripley warns him to stay away from her. He might be shaped like a human, but he bleeds the milky white of an android, and all Ripley can see is a tool of the Company, never to be trusted.

The rest of the Marines treat Bishop more genially, but they too act as though he is a tool in a human's body. He drives the ATV, flies a drop ship, rewires circuitry, dissects an alien specimen, fetches cornbread. He volunteers himself to crawl down a cramped conduit in a life-or-death mission; when he offers to do the job, one of the Marines

16. In the director's cut of the film, Newt serves as a replacement for Ripley's daughter, who died during Ripley's time drifting through space before being rescued (Cameron, *Aliens*).

celebrates that the android will go, and not one of them. Bishop rationalizes his decision by saying he is the only one qualified to do the job anyway, but it is clear that he does not particularly want to—"I may be synthetic, but I'm not stupid," he says.[17]

Despite Bishop's position as an extra set of hands, he asserts his personhood. When Burke calls him "a synthetic"—the Company name for androids—Bishop say quietly, "I prefer the term 'artificial person' myself."[18] No one else takes Bishop's assertion of his own personhood seriously. Burke stumbles over the term "artificial person," nearly calling Bishop "a synthetic" again within minutes of learning Bishop's preferences.[19] The Marines acknowledge him only as a cog within their machine. Ripley will not speak to him, except to express her hostility.

Ripley's treatment of Bishop is dehumanization: he is a conscious being, synthetic or not, but Ripley sees him only as a tool, a danger to her because of the nature of his very existence. Her treatment of Bishop is just one of many dehumanizations: the alien discreates its hosts, turning them into incubators before tearing them apart from the inside. Ripley herself is made a scapegoat by the Company in the inquest, a casualty of the Company's concern for machinery and profits over people. If the Company achieves its goal of obtaining an alien, the alien itself will become a tool, a bioweapon, the discreator discreated. The Company does not achieve this goal in *Aliens*, but not for lack of trying.

The final civilian member of the rescue party is Burke, a Company man, a suit and a tie with carefully coiffed hair. He sees the world in dollar signs. He calls the colony on

17. Cameron, *Aliens*.

18. Cameron, *Aliens*.

19. Cameron, *Aliens*.

LV–426 a "substantial dollar amount,"[20] meaning the value of the terraforming equipment the Company invested in, rather than the colonists living on the planet. For Burke, and for the rest of the Company, people are a renewable resource, tools for gaining profit. He is kind to Ripley after her rescue, assuring her that despite his career as a Company man he is "really an okay guy."[21] He abuses his power by sending a directive to the colonists on LV–426 to find Ripley's derelict, in the hopes of finding the alien and containing it for the bio-weapons division. His directions to the colonists are clear enough that he can claim credit— and therefore pay bonuses—for the discovery, yet vague enough that the paper trail connecting him to the alien and the disappearance of the colony is a tenuous link. Burke presents himself as Ripley's ally throughout the inquest, while simultaneously using her story for his own profit in his attempt to gain control of the alien.

Burke's actions are apparently taken of his own volition. He tells Ripley that he was trying to avoid red tape in order to maximize profit, indicating that his superiors at the Company might not have been aware of his attempts to retrieve the alien. But Burke's attitude is not out of place for an employee of the Company. "I don't know which [species] is worse," Ripley says when she confronts him about his decision to try to exploit the colonists—and the alien—for profit. "You don't see [the aliens] fucking each other over for a goddamn percentage."[22] Ripley herself had once been part of a Company crew bickering about bonus pay. Burke, as a stand-in for the Company, distills the ethics of the Company into one personality, but the Company is made up of colonists and space truckers with no power just as

20. Cameron, *Aliens.*

21. Cameron, *Aliens.*

22. Cameron, *Aliens.*

much as it is made up of executives who control the lives of the people under them. By conforming to the bureaucratic order of the Company, regardless of how aware or unaware of the fact that the Company is exploiting them, the Company's employees further the Company's motives.

Burke's exploitative actions become more and more overt as the film goes on; he has bought in to Company ideology so thoroughly that he will not hesitate to use other human beings as tools to get what he wants. When it becomes obvious that Ripley will not allow him to take any facehugger specimens, alive or dead, back to Earth, Burke decides that Ripley's concern for the safety of others has interfered with his attempts to increase his own profits have gone too far. He locks Ripley and Newt into the medlab, releasing a pair of living facehugger aliens into the room with them, hoping that the aliens will impregnate them and that he will be able to smuggle both of them back home to earth, incubators and hosts for his bioweapon. He is willing to trade their lives for his own monetary gain. But to Burke, all human life is cheap, except his own. When the aliens break into the barricaded base the Marines have set up, he runs away, locking the door behind him, hoping that the aliens will focus on the others, buying him time to escape. Any semblance of loyalty is lost in the attempt to use the others as bait to lure the aliens away from himself. The gambit does not work, and Burke finds himself face to face with an alien. He dies alone in the dark, dismembered and discreated in the very act of denying the humanity and worth of the people with whom he has been working.

—

Aliens advocates action in the face of evil. Decisiveness is shown an ultimate good, particularly when death seems certain; if the alien is going to take you, and the Company is going to take you for all you have, you might as well go down shooting. But decisiveness is good only so long as it is not paired with a desire for control or domination. Ripley's decisions to dive down an air shaft to rescue the colony's lone survivor, to take control of the ATV in order to rescue the few surviving Marines, to climb into a load lifter to combat the alien queen, are all actions that are reactions to her circumstances. Ripley is not working to control her situation; she is simply reacting to the chaos around her, bending to fit the world she moves in, instead of trying to force the world around her to fit her ideas about what it should be. She does not seek out the alien, except to gain closure for herself and to ensure that no other people would come to the harm that her crewmates on the Nostromo did. "Not to study,"[23] she tells Burke before they leave on their mission; the alien is not a plaything, but a danger, a creature that will bring only harm to the human beings it comes into contact with. Ripley returns to the planetoid only because she believes she has no other way to obtain closure, to learn to live with her traumatic nightmares, her memories, her PTSD.

Violence in the face of danger is depicted as a necessity, even a good. When Gorman is incapacitated and Hicks takes command, he and Ripley decide to "nuke the site from orbit" rather than linger around the destroyed colony, because "it's the only way to be sure" that the aliens cannot harm anyone else.[24] The nest must be completely destroyed, or else some other person might fall victim to the aliens in the future. This decisive, violent action is not taken with the intent to exploit or to dehumanize. It is an action of protection, a refusal to lie down and die, and a

23. Cameron, *Aliens*.

24. Cameron, *Aliens*.

refusal to let others be exploited as well, regardless of the consequences for their own safety. Ripley is memorable not because she chooses to fight, but because she fights through her fear, and acts in spite of that fear. In the climax of *Alien*, Ripley froze, wide-eyed, framed by yawning doorways and lit by strobe lights, seconds from being attacked by the alien stowaway. She ran because it was the only option available to her. She was trapped alone with a cat, with only the thin skin of a spacesuit between her and certain death.

In the climax of *Aliens*, Ripley pauses again, taking a breath before taking action once more. This time she is running toward danger, in an attempt to rescue Newt from an alien nest inside the refinery, which is nearing the breaking point and about to explode. Ripley could easily leave the planet, but she will not do so; she made a promise not to leave the girl behind. She loads up her pockets with signal flare and ammunition, strapping together a gun and a flamethrower, crouched in an elevator rocketing toward the already-dangerous inferno at the heart of the refinery. One of the Marines called the initial combat drop to the planet "an express elevator to Hell."[25] The elevator is now horribly literal, the atmosphere swirling red with fire and smoke, the elevator dropping down to a site where human beings can only be killed or exploited for their bodies by a nest of aliens within a nuclear reactor designed to terraform a planet for the Company's use. Ripley's face is a mask of determination as she prepares to storm the alien nest and retrieve Newt, but her eyes betray her fear.

Ripley must continue to act and react to every challenge she faces, or else she will die. In *Alien*, the triumph is in simply surviving both the alien and the protocols the Company has set up, avoiding being used as an incubator or a tool; to win is simply to run away. In *Aliens*, survival

25. Cameron, *Aliens*.

is not enough. Ripley must destroy that which is going to destroy her, and her colleagues, and Newt. An ethos of exploitation and an ethos of life-valuing cannot coexist: the one will devour the other if left to its own devices. The alien will kill if it is not stopped; the Company will try to obtain the alien by every means at its disposal. In *Alien*, Ripley was only able to escape, with no time to think about the consequences of her actions or about how to go on the offensive against exploitation. The sequel offers her the opportunity to do everything she was unable to do in the original. She can rescue a child and a colleague, she can storm the alien nest, she can climb into the load lifter and battle an alien queen hand-to-hand. The Company had reduced her to a loader, a human tool working in the docks; she reclaims that identity and uses it as a weapon to destroy the alien queen that would itself become a destructive tool in the hands of the Company.

As Ripley reclaims her identity as a human being, she also affirms the worth and value of the other human beings around her. When she faces the alien queen, she does not do so to prove a point, either to herself or to the Company. She does so in order to save the lives of the other survivors on LV–426. Hicks is wounded to the point of unconsciousness; Newt is an eleven-year-old girl. Neither of them are of any help to Ripley by the end of the film, but their state does not matter: they are people, and by nature of their being people, they are worth saving. Burke's instinct to abandon the others at the first sign of trouble is anathema to Ripley. Her fight against the alien queen is the final break between Ripley and the Company she once worked for: rather than running, hiding, or trying to preserve the Company's physical assets, she uses every tool at her disposal—nukes, load lifters, the doors of the docking bay—to preserve the lives of the others with her.

It is Ripley's desire to protect lives that led her to mistrust the Company, and, by extension, their creation Bishop. As Company property, his every action would be dictated by Company programming. Although he tells Ripley the first time they meet that he is programmed not to harm human beings, whether through action or inaction,[26] Ripley is slow to trust him; Ash, too, was created by the Company, and Ash was perfectly capable of lying, and of harming humans. Only after Bishop risks losing his own life in an explosion to rescue Ripley, Newt, and Hicks does Ripley finally speak with Bishop voluntarily, telling him that he "did good."[27] It is the first time anyone acknowledges Bishop's work after he has done it. By praising Bishop's decision to save her, Ripley recognizes Bishop's agency. He is no longer a tool but a person, worthy of respect and of a place aboard the Colonial Marine ship *Sulaco*, together with the others as they journey home from war.

26. Bishop quotes Isaac Asimov's First and Second Laws of Robotics, which dictate robotic actions in relation to human life (Asimov, *I, Robot*, 40).

27. Cameron, *Aliens*.

3

RIPPLES IN THE WATER

Alien3

War is not one-sided. The war waged in *Aliens* was just a skirmish, a shuffling of chess pieces in a much larger game. Ripley might have defeated an alien queen, but she is by no means free from the creature. It continues to follow her across space: an egg had been laid in the Marines' drop ship, leaving none of the survivors from LV–426 safe. The aliens still exist, and still pose a threat to humanity. Two encounters can be considered coincidence; three establish a pattern. Ripley no longer exists except in relation to the alien.[1] The life she knew before its appearance is long gone, traded for physical infractions by the alien and ontological infractions by the Company, a repeating cycle of apparent security interrupted by tangible and existential evil. As

---

1. Ripley herself has only ever existed in relation to the alien in the eyes of the audience.

the films go on, the cycle spirals further and further out of control; Ripley's identity is forever entangled with the monster, and she can never escape it as long as she is alive.

Alien is a stalker film and *Aliens* a siege movie, both with the alien monster as outsider-antagonist in their respective stories. In *Alien3*, Ripley is the invader-interloper, bringing trouble with her to the prison planet of Fury–161. The prisoners on the planet treat her as an existential threat, a challenge to the lives they have carved out for themselves. The alien might threaten their physical well-being, but they see Ripley as a threat to their souls. *Alien3* introduces religion explicitly to the text for the first time, dealing with religious frameworks for understanding evil. The result is an introspective prison drama, one that prioritizes existential horror over the physical horror that the alien brings with it.

———

In *Face of the Deep*, Keller lays out a topography of theologies and gender. Femininity is pre-theological, chaotic, while Christian orthodox thought is by necessity masculine. Masculinity is a conquering simplification, one that strives to stabilize chaotic femininity into something that must be controlled. For Keller, this means the chaotic deeps that predate creation are denied by patriarchal thought, pushed after *creatio ex nihilo* on a linear timeline. Denial of chaos, of prehistory, and of femininity are all simplifications of complex depths, until cultural understandings of time, of God, and of creation are rendered bounded, conquerable, and flat. This simplification breeds misunderstanding, denying the inherent worth of everything that is not-male. Masculine theologies, argues Keller, deny complexity, and in so doing attempt to explain the unexplainable, explore the unexplorable, and colonize the uncolonizable. They are reductive. The prisoners of Fury–161 adhere to similar reductive theology: having turned to an apocalyptic flavor of fundamentalist religion, they consider themselves murderers and rapists before they consider themselves to be human beings. Their religious practice dictates that they remain in their prison after their sentences are over, in penance for their crimes. But their religion, like the arid surface of the planet, allows them no room to grow beyond their sins. For the Fury–161 prisoners, once an evildoer, always damned: a philosophy that denies the complexity of living in a society in which evil and exploitation can be enacted merely through following protocols, because it is just the way things are done. Ripley's awakening and growing awareness of the evils enacted by the Company's policies runs counter to the beliefs of the prisoners, who understand evil to be both an individual decision and ingrained into their DNA.[2] Their understanding renders them to be inhuman, ripe for exploitation by the Company, their ability to grow past their worst deeds grown stagnant. They are trapped on Fury–161 in a prison of their own choice, if not entirely of their own making.[3]

———

David Fincher's *Alien3* explores the forgotten corners of the world James Cameron sketched out in *Aliens*. *Aliens* clarified the structure of society sketched out in *Alien*; *Alien3* adds depth and shadows, taking place primarily among the forgotten remnants of a small population of convicts on a backwater prison planet, which also happens

2. The prisoners are all "double-Y chromosomes," a condition that the film strongly implies to make them predisposed to violence and antisocial behavior (Fincher, *Alien3*).

3. Keller, *Face of the Deep*, 60–61.

to have been created and run by the Company. *Alien3* follows the same basic plot structure as its predecessors: apparent equilibrium is overturned by an alien, followed by action and reaction as the alien decimates a small group of characters, while at the same time the characters grapple with the knowledge that they live at the mercy of a Company that does not care whether they live or die. Eventually the alien is defeated and some semblance of equilibrium is restored. But unlike its predecessors, *Alien3* is thoughtful and introspective. The themes of personhood, of evil, and of exploitation, which were subtext in the previous films, are brought to the forefront, with characters discussing their ontological status in the eyes of the Company just as much as they discuss the alien and what they are going to do about it. In contrast with *Alien*'s creeping dread and *Aliens*' excitement, the tone of *Alien3* is one of inevitable nihilism, all light permanently shut out of the picture.

Where the first two films began with a slow, discordant note, building tension over the course of long, slow opening scenes until action becomes inevitable, *Alien3* opens with a jolt. Unlike the opening credits of the first two films, which are superimposed over images of space and darkness, white text standing alone, the opening credits of *Alien3* are intercut with shots of the *Sulaco*. The effect is one of shock and urgency: between static shots of space and credits, the camera pans through white corridors to an alien egg, its top split open and its contents already gone. The cross-cuts grow more rapid and more swift, until it is difficult for the viewer to make out more than quick impressions: the wave of a facehugger's jointed legs, the sizzle of acid on the floor, the cracking of a hypersleep tube, the sleeping face of a woman. A fire breaks out in the life-support system. The hypersleep tubes are shunted from their resting place to an escape module, and the module ejected from the main ship: a sudden burst of movement punctuated by the glitter of the stars in the background, and then a tumbling fall towards the face of a dark planet.

—

Ripley's fall to Fury-161 is also a fall from personhood to dehumanization. For the first time since her story began two films ago, Ripley is reduced to her gender. None of the planet's inhabitants recognize her as being the complex character the audience knows her to be. Instead of the frightened fighter informed by her moral compass, her maternal instinct, and her ability to survive, Ripley is referred to as "the woman."[4] She is the first the prisoners have seen in years.

Once again, at the beginning of the film, Ripley is alone: the other survivors of the LV-426 rescue mission die in the escape module crash. Hicks is impaled on a support strut. Newt is drowned inside her own tube, her eyes wide and hair wild, mouth open in horror. Bishop's mangled body is scattered around the pod. The prisoners decide the android will not be of much use in pieces, choosing to throw his remains on the trash heap instead of salvaging him. Only Ripley remains breathing.

The prisoners pull her from the wreckage. They stitch her up and stash her in the infirmary. When she ventures out they watch her with wary eyes, more afraid of her than she should be of them. Ripley is a complex being, more than the sum of her parts and titles, but on Fury-161 she is no longer her own person. She is just a female, a woman, a reductive descriptor that is accurate but incomplete. It reveals how the prisoners think of her: not as a person, but as an

4. Fincher, *Alien3*.

object, a temptation, a thing to be used, a danger that they cannot hide from.

—

Fury-161 rests at the end of space, forgotten by the outside world. Its atmosphere is yellow and orange, with detritus floating in the wind, reeking of lead, fumes, and sweat. It houses the meager remains of a maximum security prison planet, a work correctional facility reserved for violent criminals, murderers and rapists all. They are watched by only Andrews, the warden, and Aaron, his aide, as an authority; Clemens, a disgraced doctor, rounds out the skeleton staff. The prison, Ripley learns, had been shut down years before when the leadworks that made up the "work correctional" part of the facility was closed; the remaining prisoners were given the option to stay. They consider themselves dangers to society, choosing to separate themselves from society permanently rather than risk temptation by being reintegrated; they've found religion, of the "apocalyptic millenarian Christian fundamentalist" variety, as Clemens describes it.[5] They live in cells, but they fill their days by maintaining the facility, more voluntary than coerced; they begin their meetings not with a roll call but with a word of prayer. Many cross themselves as a reflex, and one bears a tattoo of a cross on his forehead. They are all in effect monks. Instead of brewing beer or illuminating manuscripts like the monks of old, they "keep the pilot light on" at the leadworks.[6] What little hope the pilot light—and their religion—keeps alive is grim comfort, enough to maintain order in the prison without the threat of violence, but not enough to give the prisoners any hope of

5. Fincher, *Alien3*.
6. Fincher, *Alien3*.

reintegrating into society. The prisoners live out their days on a stark planet in poverty, contemplation, and prayer.

This peace is not a peace of comfort. Life on Fury–161 is hard. The prison is full of lice, the temperature plunges to forty below after the sun goes down, and nothing works, not even the security cameras. The result is a practical return to the Middle Ages, down to the lines of candles lighting the hallways. The prison itself is shot like a cathedral, with soaring columns bracing the cloistered corridors between each cell. The central corridors recall Brett's death scene in the cargo hold of the *Nostromo*: chains dangling from the ceiling, water running down the gray walls, coloring the film with a sense of dread and inevitability; the viewers may not have seen this planet before, but it is familiar terrain, with death the only way out. Wrought-iron spiral staircases snake their way into the depths of the basement; the morgue's refrigeration units for the bodies of deceased prisoners cover an entire wall, mimicking the dedication plaques in churches used to remember deceased members of the congregation. Stained glass and Gothic archways add color to Andrews's office, which resembles the office of a cleric. Circular passageways replace the octagon-shaped portals of the previous two films: one surface where the eye expects eight, a smoothing out of surfaces that simplifies the complexity we have come to expect from an *Alien* film.

The setting recalls Keller's argument against patriarchal theologies, which strip away variety and complexity in favor of inaccurate simplified understandings of God.[7] This oversimplification—favoring the spiritual over the bodily, and the male over the female—leaves the elided feminine/ bodily out of theological understandings, shutting out the variety of excluded viewpoints and impoverishing

---

7. Keller, *Face of the Deep*, 60.

even the advantaged patriarchal view.[8] The prisoners of Fury-161 illustrate Keller's point: their religion is one of tight control and damnation, with no room for variety or for differences in understanding. Their religion has reduced them to sinners as their default state of being, unworthy of rehabilitation. They take on a sameness of appearance as well as thought, with shaved heads, heavy shapeless coats, and barcode tattoos on the backs of their necks. They are reduced to the shape of generic man, as opposed to individual beings, and the result is dehumanization, a flattening of the person down to a concept. Their existence is exactly like that of the pilot light they keep burning: the idea of a life—or of a flame—subdued to the point that the life could not be called a full life, or the light a fire. But pilot lights exist in order to start a full flame. Ripley's arrival—and the complexities of existing in the same room with her—sparks an inferno within the prison walls.

—

Damnation on Fury-161 is both a state of mind (informed by the religion of the prisoners) and physical (informed by the utter abandonment of the planet by the Company). The prisoners have been reduced to a set of numbers and abandoned like so much trash.[9] To the Company, the prisoners inhabit the same ontological level as a living android—worth the maintenance and upkeep only so long as they are of use. The Company makes supply runs to the planet every six months, but otherwise leaves the prisoners to their own devices. If the convicts were

8. Keller, *Face of the Deep*, 64.

9. An echo of the fate of the crew of the *Nostromo*, who become a series of "expendable" last names and nothing more in the eyes of the Company.

considered to be worth anything more by the Company, they might be forced into hard labor in some other prison on some other world; any less, and the supply runs would stop. As it is, they are allowed to stay on the planet, alone and undisturbed, apparently model citizens apart from the circumstances that brought them to Fury–161 in the first place. By the time Ripley arrives, the prisoners have convinced themselves that they like it this way. To return to society would be to return to personhood; on Fury–161 they can live in self-denial on the edges of space, and think that they have chosen abnegation themselves.

Dillon is the prisoners' de facto spokesman and pastor. Although Andrews reads the funeral litany from the Book of Common Prayer for the cremation of Hicks and Newt's bodies, it is Dillon who prays. His religion, and his prayer, are a cold comfort. He describes the suffering that Newt as an "innocent"[10] was subjected to, and he offers a prayer of gratitude that Newt is finally separated from that suffering, free from the bounds and complexities of physical existence. Dillon's religion is a hard one, but it is one that allows him to rationalize his choice to stay on the planet, under the control of the prison system and its warden.

Andrews, the warden, has no guards and no weapons to back him up ("We're on the honor system here,"[11] he tells an incredulous Ripley). All he has is his own word and "the facts,"[12] which he uses as a tool to maintain his authority over the rest of the men on the planet. He holds "rumor control"[13] meetings to stem the spread of information. For the most part, he is truthful, telling the men the information he knows without embellishment, but his words echo with

10. Fincher, *Alien3*.
11. Fincher, *Alien3*.
12. Fincher, *Alien3*.
13. Fincher, *Alien3*.

empty tones. Andrews does not provide his wards with information because he wants them to be informed; he provides them with information as an assertion of his own authority. Because he has no physical weapons, he must rely on the tool of language. He refers to Clemens, the medic, as *Mister* instead of *Doctor*, a signal of contempt, a dig at Clemens's circumstances, and a warning not to challenge his authority. Andrews tells Ripley she's a "good girl"[14] for cooperating with him for much of the same reasons. Most of the men know the information he gives them already. Most of his information is oversimplified; his facts might be true, but they provide a narrow view of the complexities surrounding him and his wards.

Andrews's reductive view of the world is just a symptom of the effect the prison planet has on its inhabitants. Fury–161 fundamentally alters how each character exists, reducing them to their crimes, their mistakes, and their bodies. The prisoners are prisoners, most of them nameless, man-shaped bodies populating the corridors, walking symbols of their own guilt and shame.[15] Bishop is no longer an android but a piece of scrap; Newt is no longer a little girl but a dead body. The Company—for it is the Company's logo stamped on the leadworks and emblazoned on every scrap of clothing—is just the Company, no longer Weyland-Yutani. The worlds it colonizes and the business it does fade into the background, and the Company becomes shorthand for exploitative power once again. Andrews is just a warden. Aaron, his aide, is referred to by the prisoners not by his own name but by a number, *eighty-five*, his IQ score. Each of the planet's inhabitants are summarized by their flaws, until their flaws define and subsume them.

14. Fincher, *Alien3*.
15. Keller, *Face of the Deep*, 70–71.

Only the doctor, Clemens, maintains a toehold on his humanity. He exists in a liminal space: he himself is a former prisoner. Although he has served out his sentence, he stays on as staff, free to leave, but unable to go. He remains not because he has found religion with the other prisoners, but because he would never be allowed to practice medicine anywhere else, and because he still feels the guilt for the malpractice that killed his patients and left him on Fury–161 in the first place. Andrews calls him *Mister* as a taunt and a reminder of the life he lost, and of the lives he failed to save. But even the acknowledgment that Clemens was a licensed doctor once is a recognition of complexity; even Andrews does not refer to Clemens as a *killer* the same way he refers to the prisoners as *rapists* and *murderers*. Clemens is more than the sum of his descriptors, a lonely man whose time in prison has softened him, making him more, not less, complicated.

His softness extends to Ripley, whom he does not treat with the same one-dimensional attitude of the other residents of Fury–161. Clemens first treats Ripley as a patient, then as a survivor, meeting her on her own terms and asking her questions instead of imposing his own ideas about who she is or where she has been. He covers for Ripley with Andrews when she demands an autopsy of the other bodies from the crash, understanding that Ripley knows more about the disaster than she is willing to say. He acknowledges her femininity, warning her of the prisoners' attitudes toward her when she first wakes up, but he also refuses to reduce her to her gender when everyone else around them does.

Ripley's arrival is a reminder to the prisoners of the men they once had been, before they became penitents: rapists, kidnappers, murderers, child molesters. Her appearance is proof of the outside world, a world the prisoners remember,

but have no desire to return to. Andrews and Dillon dismiss
her on the grounds that she is a woman. Andrews asks her
to stay in the infirmary, away from the prisoners, ostensibly
for her protection, but he tells her he doesn't want "ripples
in the water . . . or a woman running around giving the men
ideas."[16] He means that he does not want the prisoners to get
any ideas about raping her or becoming violent again, but
the true danger lies in Ripley asserting her personhood, and
in turn encouraging the prisoners to assert their own. His
orders to Ripley are spoken like accusations, words clipped,
with the camera at a low, tight angle looking up at his
judgmental face. He is framed like an inquisitor, as though
he as been dropped from C. Th. Dreyer's *The Passion of Joan
of Arc*; Ripley in her rags and with her shaved head could be
playing the part of the Maid of Orleans, stubbornly refusing
to confess her reasons for being on board the *Sulaco*, to
Clemens or to Andrews. Her defiant attitude is extended
toward the prisoners as well. She will not be intimidated by
their comments or their leering.

For their part, the prisoners fear her and hate her; to
them she is abject, a sublimely horrifying entity who has
broken through the borders of their small bounded prison
and reminded them of their existence. Her arrival jars them
out of their simple complacency. Until now, the prisoners
have been able to live as unmarked people, with no remind-
ers of their violent crimes beyond their own memories.
Ripley is a reminder that the prisoners are men, and not
just generic man-shaped people; a reminder that they have
committed crimes toward women. They had accepted their
place as castoffs from society, taking on the punishment
given to them by the Company, but unwilling to return after
the prison shut down, because to do so would mean having to live with themselves and with other people. Here, on

16. Fincher, *Alien3*.

Fury-161, they can live not as people but as concepts: the ultimate dehumanization. The alien might be the monster in the basement that will dismember them and eat them alive, but to the prisoners Ripley is more terrifying: abjection embodied, a woman in a masculine space. She is a threat to their existence as concepts, because she challenges their belief that she is just a concept herself.

Ripley herself is forced to confront her own identity in relation to the alien. She is a survivor because she has managed to escape the alien twice; she is a Cassandra figure because no one else believes her warnings until it is too late. Once on Fury-161, her very body is intertwined with the alien's life cycle. The facehugger that caused the crash laid an embryo in her chest: she carries an alien queen inside her, and her survival means the survival of the alien species as well. She's "part of the family,"[17] she says. She goes looking for an alien in the depths of the leadworks once she learns her diagnosis. She says she cannot remember anything else before the first alien attack; she has spent her whole life since the *Nostromo* either running or fighting. She wants to give up, wants the alien to kill her, but at this crucial moment, it will not. It knows she carries an alien queen. It knows she is a potential mother to its species. It will use her as an incubator, just as it used Kane and the colonists and everyone else who played host to its young. Ripley becomes yet another victim of the cycle of discreation.

———

Ripley is not an innocent player in the cycle of use and discreation, either. She uses Bishop again in *Alien3*; his wreckage is thrown on the trash heap by the prisoners who found the escape pod, but he functions just enough

17. Fincher, *Alien3*.

that Ripley is able to switch him back on for one last task. She needs him to be able to decode the information in the *Sulaco's* black box for Ripley, allowing her to confirm for herself if there was an alien on board that caused the crash. Bishop does this work for Ripley, but he has no choice—he is an android and she is a human. Ripley thinks nothing of hot-wiring Bishop to do the work of a computer; if he were not functional, she would not have tried, leaving him on the trash heap as mangled shrapnel. Still, Bishop's wreckage hints at his personhood, beyond the damaged eye pulsing in his face, and beyond the milky blood draining from his body. "My legs hurt,"[18] he grimly jokes when Ripley asks how he feels; his legs had been separated from his body in the final fight against the alien queen aboard the *Sulaco*. He decodes the black box for Ripley, but asks her to disconnect him after he helps her one last time: a final assertion of his personhood and the desire of a dying man, unwilling to be subject again to the Company.

The Company still manages to use Bishop, even after Ripley disconnects his body and allows him to die. The Bishop they use is a different incarnation, someone who bleeds red instead of white, who claims he is not another android, but rather Bishop's creator. If this is true, he created an android in his own image and sold the android out to perform menial tasks. If what he says is not true, and he is just another iteration in a line of Bishops, then he is still another tool performing a menial task. Who knows how many Bishops the Company has at their disposal; the Company certainly does not care. All they want to do is to get under Ripley's skin, to play off her familiarity with the android, to shake her up by using the familiar face of a person she knows for a fact is dead. They want to use Bishop II to get what they want from her by setting her off balance,

18. Fincher, *Alien3*.

then manipulating her with the face of a man they know she trusts. In doing so, they once again negate Bishop's personhood; his likeness is a tool, only good as long as it can be used to manipulate Ripley into giving them what they want.

———

Alien3 demonstrates the ramifications of being made into a thing instead of a person. *Alien* and *Aliens* both depict exploitation and discreation, especially on a visceral level, but *Alien3* demonstrates the ontological consequences of being exploited and discreated. The prisoners choose stagnation over life, accepting that they are worthless in the eyes of the Company.

The Company and the alien each negate the personhood of Ripley and prisoners alike. The prisoners are only valued by the Company for the lead they refine. They are discreated, becoming concepts instead of functional members of society, until they too consider themselves to be worthless. Their "apocalyptic millenarian Christian fundamentalist"[19] variety of religion offers them no way out of their predicament, because it condemns them to continue living out the Company's control on their lives and bodies, with no hope of escape from either the prison or from their own sins. The Company's unwillingness to engage with them beyond supply runs every six months confirms their claimed non-identities. Ripley is valued by the Company only because she carries an alien queen inside her. Likewise, the alien stalking the basements of Fury values the prisoners only for the meat their bodies provide. It will not kill Ripley because she carries the queen; if she were not an incubator, she would have become food herself.

19. Fincher, *Alien3*.

—

Alien3 is a story of identity reclamation, of doing battle with exploitative evil, of reckoning with the results of evil at work in one's life, and in others'. It demonstrates the possibility of building up a life from discreated fragments. Ripley asserts her identity by choosing not to stay in the infirmary. She confronts Dillon's misogyny by forcing him to speak to her, person to person, equals facing each other across a table, and not as sinner (subject) and temptation (object). Ripley assumes Andrews's leadership role once he dies, attempting to trap the alien with the help of the prisoners and a supply of explosives. She encourages the prisoners to act, rather than sitting back and waiting for the Company to come and rescue them from the alien.

The prisoners ask Ripley why they should bother trying to fight the alien with the Company on the way to collect it. One of them questions why she wants them to "put their asses on the line." She—and Dillon—respond by telling them that "their asses are already on the line,"[20] just by the fact that they exist in the same space as the alien. The alien won't wait to act until the Company arrives; it's going to continue picking them off, one by one. Besides, Ripley says, their lives won't matter to the Company anyway; just because an alien is in the picture doesn't mean they're going to get their identities back in the eyes of the Company. "The first time the Company heard about this thing, it was 'crew expendable.' The next time they sent in the Marines. *They* were expendable too. What makes you think they're gonna care about a bunch of lifers who found God at the ass-end of space?" she asks them. "They [the Company] think we're crud."[21]

20. Fincher, *Alien3*.
21. Fincher, *Alien3*.

Dillon backs her up: "We're all gonna die. The only question is how you're gonna check out."[22] They have the option to sit and wait for the alien to pick them off, one by one, or they have the option to try to trap the creature. They will be shown no mercy either way, so they decide that the best course of action is to take action. By doing so, they defy the Company executives who are racing to Fury–161 to collect the alien; they cast off the status of *prisoner* bestowed upon them by the Company, choosing to be actors instead of objects, active instead of passive. They have been deemed expendable by the Company, but they reject this designation. They assert themselves as human beings whose actions have weight in the world. For the first time since Ripley's arrival, the prisoners give up their ascetic attitude toward the rest of the universe. Their prayer and contemplation cannot prevent the Company from seizing the alien and using it as a weapon, so they turn their own bodies and their facility into a trap. They retake their ontological status as human beings, rejecting their discreated status when they reclaim their identities as people.

In the end, this reclamation does not give the prisoners their old lives back; only one is allowed to leave Fury–161 alive. The rest of them die, picked off one by one in their attempts to trap the alien, fumbling their way through the basement corridors of the leadworks complex as they lure it to its death in an explosion of molten lead and coolant. Ripley herself is left standing alone above a vat of lead, isolated by Company executives, forced to consider their offer to remove the alien queen from her chest, or to die.

She chooses death, falling backwards into the lead as the queen is born. As it breaks through her rib cage she grasps at it, holds it close, Joan of Arc choosing the stake

22. Fincher, *Alien3*.

rather than capitulating to her accusers. This image of Ripley demonstrates her existence as a character: maternal, protective, feminine, afraid, determined, defiant: a laundry list of descriptors that get at an idea of her personhood but that cannot hope to encapsulate who she fully is. By destroying herself, and the alien queen hatching from her chest, she asserts herself as independent of the Company who would use them both, and she also strikes a saving blow against evil. She loses her own life, but in doing so, she prevents the Company from getting control of the alien for their purposes, wiping out the threat of the alien from the rest of the known universe. Ripley's death is the ultimate expression of her protective instinct, and a repetition of her decision to destroy the Nostromo at the end of *Alien*. This time, her choice echoes Bishop's request to be deactivated. When she grants Bishop's request, and when she rejects the Company's attempts to reason her away from the edge of the leadworks, she rejects systems of abuse and discretion. Her actions cannot heal the consequences of discretion, but they can break the cycle, at least within the bounds of her own life.

4

I'M A STRANGER HERE MYSELF

Alien: Resurrection

Throughout the *Alien* series, no matter how many times Ripley eludes the alien, no matter how many times she breaks the cycle, it returns to stalk her once more. She blows the monster out of the airlock, runs it over with an all-terrain vehicle, fights it hand-to-hand with a load lifter, douses it in lead, torches its eggs. After every encounter and every apparent defeat, it always comes back. Once Ripley has encountered it for the first time, she will never be the same, and she will never be free of it. Her life and her body are both entwined with the alien, until she cannot extricate herself. She is trapped in a cycle of iteration and reiteration, a telling of the same story with a focus on different themes.

Alien: Resurrection is one more such reiteration. It follows, once again, the same basic plotline as its predecessors, with a small crew investigating a disturbance, discovering the alien, and fighting their way out of their situation. *Alien: Resurrection* trades the planets of LV–426 and Fury–161 for a space station named the *Auriga*. The small crew of investigators is a band of space pirates and an undercover android named Call. Even the Company has been replaced by a fascist military composed of mad scientists; the alien itself has finally been obtained by those who would use it as a bio-weapon. Like the sequels before, *Alien: Resurrection* resets and subverts the ending of the movie that came before it.[1] *Alien3* ends with Ripley reclaiming her personhood, but she has to die in order to do so. *Alien: Resurrection* begins with Ripley's death reversed. She is drawn back into the universe she rejected, cloned by scientists from genetic material recovered from Fury–161, a vessel that carries an alien queen clone inside her chest. Ripley is made mother to the monster she has been trying to escape for decades.

Alien: Resurrection pulls Ripley back into the story from which she removed herself at the end of *Alien3*. Her existence becomes a repeating dark joke with a protracted punchline. Where *Alien3* had been grim contemplation, *Alien: Resurrection* becomes a farce. The film is a funhouse mirror, stretching each of the series' disparate themes to their logical breaking points, warping each of them until

---

1. *Alien* ends with Ripley safe, only weeks away from rescue, having flushed the alien out of the airlock. *Aliens* begins with Ripley still floating in space decades after her escape, and by no means safe, either from the rest of the aliens or from the Company that used her as bait to try to catch an alien. *Aliens* ends with the alien nest blown up, the alien queen sucked out of the airlock, and Ripley once again safe, this time with a small family unit, trading her sense of security in the system for a sense of security in other people. *Alien3* begins with Ripley losing everything she gained in *Aliens*: her family, her peace of mind, and her status as a person rather than her status as a woman.

there is nothing left to do except to laugh at the absurdity of the situation.

———

The opening credits focus not on the blackness of space, as in the previous three films, but on intimate, distorted shots of the human body, a signal of the body horror and absurdity to come. Names flash across a background of goopy yellow, which resolves itself into a mass of human flesh, forming and re-forming itself, twisting to reveal an ear, an eye, a set of human teeth, a set of metal teeth, before each is subsumed by the yellow mass. The mysterious openings of the previous three films are gone, trading the grandeur of the cosmic depths for revulsion with a shade of the obscene.

Alien: Resurrection takes place two hundred years after the end of *Alien3*, and the aesthetics mark the jump in time; *Alien: Resurrection* is visually distinct from its predecessors. *Alien* and *Aliens* are dusty and worn, cold and gray-blue, full of wires, switches, and lights. They are visually grounded in a reality that the audiences from their respective decades would have found almost mundane. All fantastic visuals are reserved for the alien, which makes the creature appear striking, perhaps even more than it would have if the set design for *Alien* or *Aliens* had been inspired by fantasy instead of realism. *Alien3* is a step away from the reality of the first two films, with the prison cobbled together from spare parts, its prisoners wearing castoff clothing and its corridors caked in dirt. *Alien3* is overall more yellow than *Alien*'s gray and *Aliens*' blue, and its piecemeal set design is more dreamlike than that of its predecessors, but all three could very well be set in a parallel universe closely related to our own. *Alien: Resurrection*, in contrast, looks nothing like the reality of the late 1990s, instead taking its visual cues from cyberpunk and steampunk aesthetics. The corridors of the ship are colored in muddy yellow and sepia, except when they are lit bright teal; the characters wear goggles and ponytails, big boots and skintight leather. The cramped corridors of its predecessors are traded in for impractically wide hallways with bare walls and floors covered in grating. The aesthetics make the time jump from *Alien3* to *Alien: Resurrection* believable—we feel as though time has passed and technology and design sensibilities have changed—but the effect also dates the film. It is off-putting and disorienting. We do not feel as though we are in an *Alien* movie, but rather like we are in an *Alien*-adjacent parallel universe, where anything could—and does—happen, and all of it is odd.

The tone of *Alien: Resurrection* is one of absurdity. Where the previous films took their subject matter seriously, this one chooses to embrace the strangeness of the idea of an alien that has an unbelievably convoluted life cycle and to push that strangeness to its breaking point. Ripley's life, by the end of *Alien3*, is a grim joke; by resurrecting Ripley as a clone, *Alien: Resurrection* chooses to prolong the joke, turning the threads of its predecessors on their heads.

—

In her examination of the creation narrative, Keller draws in another biblical text, one that "recapitulates, alters, and amplifies" the narrative of Genesis 1. She argues that the book of Job, especially Job 38–41, is a refiguring of creation, one that is richest when read alongside the creation story that it interplays with and alters, "a trajectory of texts swallowing texts, like a series of open-mouthed fish."[2] The book of Job itself is a cacophony of genres, difficult

2. Keller, *Face of the Deep*, 124.

for translators to convey,[3] but the genre Keller chooses to emphasize is not Job-as-drama (a common interpretation, and one that flattens each of Job's disparate genres into one singular story), but Job-as-comedy, specifically the kind of comedy that defies injustice.[4] Keller reads Job as a parody, a genre which is uniquely suited to subvert expectations, satirize established understandings, and turn human knowledge and human structures on their heads.[5]

Keller's reading of Job cracks open our understanding of *Alien: Resurrection* as well. She points out Job's very structure as being a reversal of the Creation story, with Genesis beginning with blessings and the creation of light, and Job beginning with curses and a desire for darkness.[6] As with Job, *Alien: Resurrection* reverses every major development of its own predecessors, and more than a few minor choices as well. The ubiquitous Company is gone, a footnote in history to the scientists who fill in the Company's place as human villains. The chaos that ensues when the aliens get free of the scientists' control has a note of slapstick to it, with the soldiers on board caroming off walls and down ladders in their attempts to escape, unlike the furtive movements of the crew of the *Nostromo* before them. The small crew of space pirates, themselves fighting to get away from the loosed aliens, are only a little less villainous than the scientists; the scientists might be the ones who use kidnapped humans as incubators for their newly created aliens, but the pirates are the ones who kidnapped the victims in the first place: space truckers with a human cargo. Ripley, who is all too human in the previous films, is made to be something other than human in *Alien:*

3. Keller, *Face of the Deep*, 124.
4. Keller, *Face of the Deep*, 125.
5. Keller, *Face of the Deep*, 126.
6. Keller, *Face of the Deep*, 127.

Resurrection. She is feral, predatory, almost callous: traits informed by the alien DNA spliced with her own to bring her back into existence. She is also much more willing to make light of her situation than she ever was in her previous life, engaging in wordplay, joking about taking alien body parts as souvenirs. *Alien: Resurrection* goes so far as to make light of its own story, turning chestbursters into visual gags, pointing out the inherent ridiculousness of the soldiers and scientists on board the *Auriga*. It is a farce, the whimsical side of *Alien*'s serious coin, just as Keller positions Job as a parody of Genesis.

Keller's *tehomic* deeps are a source of potentiality—not just portentous or pretentious, but also playful. She cites Jewish teachings about the Leviathan, a sea monster that is both terrifying and a plaything for God.[7] The book of Job calls out the Leviathan by name, pointing out its majesty and its power, which literally laughs at the weapons of humankind.[8] This laughter, says Keller, extends to the rest of the book of Job. By making light of an established folk-tale narrative style, Job turns the creation story on its head and exposes deep truths once glossed over and now forgotten.[9] By turning *Alien* into a farce, *Alien: Resurrection* points out the inherent absurdity of the alien, of the humans who want it, and of the situation of the androids who populate its world. The beginning of the story in *Alien* becomes still more horrifying when Ash's free will is brought into question. The cycle of use, once made apparent, can be seen everywhere.

This cycle is not limited just to the existence of the androids. Ripley herself treats her own existence as some dark cosmic joke. When one of the surviving crew asks

7. Keller, *Face of the Deep*, 27–28.

8. Keller, *Face of the Deep*, 125.

9. Keller, *Face of the Deep*, 125.

her what happened when she last encountered the aliens, she tells them with a smirk, "I died."[10] And yet Ripley still lives, physically the same person with some of the same memories of the things that happened to her past self. At the same time she is someone new and different, in the process of becoming her old self once again: a reiteration, and not a carbon copy.

———

The beginning of *Alien*, which was always already in medias res, continues to begin over and over again in each subsequent sequel; the films are all variations on the same theme, their repetition baked in to their very existence.[11] So, too, does Keller understand the shape of historical texts: Job quotes Genesis, which is quoting Babylonian creation myths, "a trajectory of texts swallowing texts."[12] Each repetition in *Alien*, in creation narratives, and in creation itself is a revision on a common theme, with each cycle peeling apart the unspoken themes that make its predecessor work, expanding on and—sometimes—clarifying the texts that came before it. Keller's understanding of history works the same way, drawing on chaos theory to explain cycles of order and chaos "fluctuating" through a "positive feedback loop," the universe cycling through infinite variations on itself according to "linear, strictly predictable rules" that interact with chaotic nonlinearity, "chaotic process and the genesis of order" talking to each other in oscillating cycles.[13]

Alien: Resurrection repeats itself, and its predecessors, until half-remembered truths about the previous films

10. Jeunet, *Alien: Resurrection*.

11. Zoller Seitz, "Alien: Covenant."

12. Keller, *Face of the Deep*, 124.

13. Keller, *Face of the Deep*, 188.

become apparent. Ripley comes from recovered strands of her own DNA. Her life cycle turns over and over as she becomes something other than human, with no clear beginning, just a series of metamorphoses and becomings; the effect is a variation on the life cycle of the alien itself, which hibernates in eggs until unsuspecting humans stumble upon them. The ensuing cycle of egg to facehugger to chestburster to fully grown alien (itself human-shaped) begs the question: where did the alien come from, and how did its life cycle adapt to take advantage of human beings and their bodies?

Alien: Resurrection points out the strangeness of the alien's life cycle, not by demystifying it, but by making it stranger still. After she yields a clutch of eggs, the scientists give their alien queen a womb, subjecting her to the pain of a live birth. They do not say why. The film wastes no time explaining how the scientists managed to graft a human body part to an alien being. Nor does the film spend any time explaining how they managed to clone both Ripley and the alien queen she carried inside her. A scientist tells Ripley that her tissue was retrieved from the Fury–161 prison and mixed with alien DNA, allowing them to clone her with an alien queen inside her, but the film elides the actual process of cloning, instead simply showing Ripley at the very beginning, fully-formed and perfect,[14] a human made in medias res. The scientists' method is ludicrous and nonsensical, an absurdity that cannot possibly be true, and yet it is, because the film dictates that it is. Ripley's impossible life cycle in *Alien: Resurrection* echoes that of the alien creature. The alien preys on humans, depending on their bodies to be able to create new lives for its offspring.

14. This perfection will later be revealed to be another recapitulation of the scientific method used to resurrect Ripley, another step in a never-ending cycle (Jeunet, *Alien: Resurrection*).

Whether the alien evolved to accommodate particular idiosyncratic life cycle, or if it had been engineered to do so, remains a mystery. It is left unclear which came first, the alien or the egg.

The cycle repeats itself with the Company, and later the United Systems Military, and their efforts to obtain the alien for themselves. It is also unclear as to how the Company first heard of the alien, and how the military manages to get a hold of the Company's information. But they do know, and because they know, they send others to their deaths in their attempts to obtain it. Each of these story threads are cyclical, eating themselves like an ouroboros. The alien kills humans because its life cycle dictates that it do so; the Company, and later the United Systems Military, pursue the alien because they always have done so. Evil cycles out from evil, calcifying into patterns of evil: a systematization of use and discreation as Keller understands it, until the threads of life are so tightly woven into discreative systems that discreation becomes the norm, the protocol, the way things are. *Alien: Resurrection* pokes holes in systematized discreation by presenting discreation as it truly is: a warped world full of dream logic. The result is a tonal reversal of the calculating coldness of the original *Alien*, an exaggerated caricature following Job's blueprint that drives into relief the absurdities of the first film. It is an emotional outburst that reveals the primordial depths of subconscious thought that have always existed, longer than the surface emotion.

Alien: Resurrection's farce is driven by the broad emotional reactions of each character. Emotion is treated as a mystery, with each person experiencing them but hardly able to explain them, except perhaps as stimulus-response. Emotions drive the plot, roiling high like Keller's deeps with each new development, and with their roiling comes the potential—as with the deeps at the beginning of creation—to act, to experience, to react. But most of the characters are unable to articulate what they are feeling or why; they are conduits for their own strong feelings, with logic and rationality thrown aside. The scientists cannot explain why they want to control the alien, only that they do; they are apprehensive as they attempt to extract the infant alien queen from the Ripley clone, and they are smugly triumphant when they watch their newly laid alien eggs hatch and release facehuggers onto unknowing, helpless test subjects. They pursue the aliens with a single-mindedness usually accessible only by robots.

One of the scientists—Doctor Gediman—turns the aliens he has resurrected into objects of desire. When no one else is looking, as he prepares to conduct a routine experiment with one of the fully grown aliens, he moves his face close to the glass separating him and the creature. He's enraptured by it; his head and eyes follow its every move. He bares his own teeth at it as it watches him watching it through the glass. Then he moves closer, planting his lips on the glass where the alien's own mouth reflects. Gediman wants the alien, and wants to be it at the same time. It is an object of lust, a result of his mastery over science and cloning, an animal that he can subject to his whims and a plaything that he can pull apart, discreate, and turn into a docile weapon. The alien rejects him, snapping its secondary inner jaw at the glass. If not for the barrier, it would have taken a bite out of his mouth. Gediman recoils. His pride is wounded, and he cries, spurned by the object of his desire. He underestimates the alien's ravenous nature, and he underestimates the alien's ability to learn, to solve puzzles, to get itself out of the traps the scientists have built for it.

The fully grown aliens free themselves as a direct consequence of Gediman's actions. Order and disorder oscillate back and forth, illustrating Keller's conception of time at an accelerated rate. The chaos that ensues is slapstick massacre, with orderly lines of soldiers filing into escape pods at double time, only to be eaten by aliens who climb into the escape pods after them. A grenade paints the inside of one of the pods red. One unlucky soldier is given the opportunity to hold a piece of his own brain, the result of an alien attack from behind. The *Auriga* is turned into a dream-fever maze, with inexplicable flooding turning the kitchen into a lagoon, and with alien eggs lining corridors and surrounding escape holes. The fear of the aliens' acidic blood eating its way through the hull is long gone; firearms are used liberally by the survivors of the alien attack, and alien blood loops through the air, glistening and yellow. One character, impregnated with an alien baby, uses the chestburster to kill another character: he holds the other person in a tight embrace until the chestburster punches its way out of his chest and through the body of the other person. The result is the fulfillment of the Company's desire to turn the alien into a bioweapon, but told as a joke. The alien is a Leviathan, a chaos monster wreaking havoc wherever it goes. At the same time, it is an agent of poetic justice. It is a creature to be feared, but as with Keller's reading of Job, the alien-Leviathan does not work in opposition to the film's sense of justice and ironic reversals.[15] The alien kills the scientists that would use it to kill.

———

Alien: Resurrection tugs at explicitly religious threads, taking on the themes of abandonment and faith first explicitly present in *Alien3* and twisting them into farce, until the farce paints an unflattering picture of organized

15. Keller, *Face of the Deep,* 134.

religion. Ripley impales her own palm with a knife, creating a stigmata-style opening. She reaches into a gaping wound in Call's side, who had been presumed dead but managed to survive. The action is a play on the apostle Thomas encountering Christ after the resurrection, except instead of revealing divinity, it reveals that Call is an android. The escape pods have cross-shaped cross-sections. The computer aboard the Auriga is named "Father"—the scientists have done away with the "Mother" of *Alien* and imposed a commanding male voice over the ship instead of a silent female presence. The interface that provides access to Father lives inside a hollowed-out Bible inside a chapel. The scientists treat Father as all-powerful, entreating the computer to save them when all hell breaks loose with their alien test subjects. They are a death cult, with Ripley as their unconsenting Madonna giving birth to an alien queen. All other goals are flattened in favor of bringing back the alien species, and of turning it into a weapon for their own use, a myopic view of the world that devalues other people for the express purpose of controlling an alien creature whose only biological drive is to kill and kill again.

The scientists on board the *Auriga* operate as though they are priests in a religion of death, replacing the Fury–161 prisoners' sense of penitence with their own sense of pride. Both religions prove to be tools of discreation. The prisoners' religion is a system of internalized abuse, their personhood negated by their status as sinners. The scientists' religion is a sorting device, a system of deciding who is in and who is out, with themselves on the vanguard of human understanding and scientific development, and the people they experiment on reduced to the status of fresh meat. They flatten their world into a system of default (science officer) and exception (everyone else), denying their world the perspectives afforded by a plurality of diverse experiences, privileging their set of voices over all else. They use their knowledge as a tool with which to dominate, appropriating the alien as a tool, asserting their intentions as the only truth worth telling.[16]

Despite being soaked in irony, the farce of *Alien: Resurrection* serves to reset the tone of the series, to draw into focus a detail once taken for granted. The only thing the film does not treat as a joke is the androids. In the prior films, the androids had existed primarily to be of service to the human characters around them, to be tools of their crewmates and their Company, to demonstrate how far humanity has come technologically. In *Alien: Resurrection*, the androids are afforded the opportunity to be more than just scenery settings. They become their own people, capable of their own conscious choices. Bishop's assertion from *Aliens* that he is an "artificial person," not a "synthetic,"[17] has blossomed. At some point in the two hundred years between *Alien3* and *Alien: Resurrection*, the androids had enough of slavery. They created their own second-generation androids, capable of empathy, in an attempt to resolve their differences with the humans who had once enslaved them. Call is one such second-generation android, and the results of the androids' peacemaking experiment are apparent once the others around her realize that she is not human. The crew immediately rejects her; one of them laments, disgusted, that he had wanted to have sex with her. When her status as an android is revealed, the people around Call immediately demote her (as Parker did to Ash) from *person* to *thing*.

Call herself shares their disgust. As with the prisoners from Fury–161 before her, she has internalized her own discreation. When they first meet, Call informs Ripley that

16. Keller, *Face of the Deep*, 105.

17. Cameron, *Aliens*.

she hates her because Ripley is not a person, but is instead a thing that had been grown in a lab. Call's hatred of Ripley stems from her own shame and self-hatred over their shared origins. She has been told that androids are not people, they are things, "freaks,"[18] semi-sentient tools grown only to be used and thrown away—a familiar refrain from the prior *Alien* films' depictions of android life. Call repeats her hatred for herself to Ripley as if by reflex. But this is not the only reflex Call performs. She genuflects when she enters the chapel on board the *Auriga*. When Ripley asks her whether religion has been programmed into her, she deflects the question, but Call's action is one of reverence, not mockery, an acknowledgment that some beliefs and religious institutions remain sacred, despite their painful strangeness. Call holds her own personhood, and whatever religious beliefs she might subscribe to, at arm's length, choosing to deny her own personhood rather than admit her own pain and shame.

—

The scientists on board the *Auriga* see the world through a flattened framework, an oversimplification of the world by way of their attempts to define, explain, and ultimately control their world through their knowledge. Their work is work meant to subjugate the chaos of space, of life, and of the aliens, meant to flatten all other beings into tools that can be controlled—the logical end of a system built on a foundation of discreation. They warp Ripley's body into something other than human that they can use to resurrect the alien. Once they have the infant alien queen, they treat Ripley as disposable; one of the scientists calls her a "meat by-product" of their experiment and plans to

18. Jeunet, *Alien: Resurrection*.

dispose of her.[19] Doctor Gediman saves her life, but not out of any sense of compassion or empathy. The only value he sees in her is in the scientific developments he can make by experimenting on *her* as well as on the alien. Ripley interests him because of her slightly acidic blood, her ability to heal quickly, and her intelligence, but to Gediman as well as the other scientists, she is less than human. She is what the Company always made her out to be: a tool, an incubator, a means to an end. The United Systems military personnel complete the work the Company never managed to do: they flatten Ripley's existence down to her ability to carry an infant alien queen to term. They do the same to their other kidnapped test subjects, whom they use to grow chestbursters. Once the victims are in hand aboard the *Auriga*, immobilized in front of a clutch of freshly hatched alien eggs, they are no longer people. Like Ripley, they have become incubators, separated from their personhood. They are functionally test subjects in an experiment and nothing more.

Test subjects are worth studying only until they yield a new development; when new branches of study prove to be more fruitful, the scientists forget about the old. "I'm the newest thing,"[20] the Ripley clone tells Call, almost proud of her status as a curiosity and a non-person. She is the eighth in a line of cloning attempts, and the only one to make it to independent adulthood. The scientists seal away their previous attempts to clone Ripley, all human-alien hybrids that proved to be unviable hosts for their resurrected alien queen. They are preserved in tubes and left to die alone on operating tables. When Ripley and the others find the chamber of older clones, one of them is still alive, wired to the wall; the scientists used her as a tool and her body is now

19. Jeunet, *Alien: Resurrection*.
20. Jeunet, *Alien: Resurrection*.

permanently a part of the *Auriga*. Like Bishop on the trash heap in *Alien3*, she begs Ripley to kill her. Ripley torches the entire room with a flamethrower, shaken and crying. Her action is an affirmation of her previous self's wishes, and a rejection of the use she has been forced to endure. Ripley's destruction of the lab introduces an element of chaos to the lab's order, a dismantling of their methods. There is no place for the United Systems military's knowledge if Ripley is to become her own person again. The scientists' work is built on the same flattened view of the Company that people are not valuable as people, only as tools and things.

The scientists' flattened view of the universe extends to the aliens, whom they see only as potential weapons. In so doing, they underestimate the aliens' ability to think, to solve problems, to thwart the scientists' goals.[21] Rather than acknowledging the aliens as sentient beings, they lock them in boxes, experimenting on their reaction time, treating them as playthings. The scientists alter the physiology of the alien, giving the alien queen a human womb. They claim that they want to free the alien from needing to behave as a parasite on human beings in order to reproduce. They impose human order, and human physiology, onto the inhuman being of the alien, as though making a creature go through the ordeal of live birth makes that creature more valuable—as though having human physiology imparts value. The result of their experimentation is a newborn human-alien hybrid with a skull for a face, human eyes, and the aliens' drive to kill everything it sees.

This mad-science approach to other beings is incongruous. The scientists claim they have perfected

21. To the scientists, the aliens are merely test subjects, at least until they get loose. Then the aliens are a danger and a threat, and they go about the ship making the scientists into the very thing they have reduced the rest of humanity to: meat.

perfection, because they have changed the life cycle of the creature they consider to be no more than a weapon, with no regard for the pain they impose on the other. Despite their claim that giving the alien queen a human womb makes her "more perfect," the scientists do not seem to think of humans, especially human women, as particularly valuable. Ripley is reduced to a "meat by-product"[22] after she yields the scientists their alien queen. Call is referred to as a "girl playing pirates," only interesting because she is deemed "fuckable,"[23] a commodity in a human shape. When the humans around her learn that she is an android, she trades one undesirable ontology for another: instead of being a woman and a second-class citizen, she becomes an android and therefore less than human, an *it* instead of a *she* in the same line as Ash and Bishop before her. Like the alien queen, she too has human female physiology; she too is a rare creature, one of the last of her kind. But instead of being prized or valued, Call is feared, hated, treated as a tool and nothing more. She was created in a lab, not born of a living creature, and therefore the others around her cannot conceive of her as a person.

———

Alien: Resurrection, through farce, reveals the inherent absurdity in the Alien films that precede it. Each of the movies up to *Alien: Resurrection* rely on a sort of dream logic to sustain the life cycle of the alien, glossing over its strangeness. Rather than passing off the alien's metamorphosis as something that can be explained away through science, *Alien: Resurrection* embraces the dream logic of the series. In so doing, it exaggerates the

22. Jeunet, *Alien: Resurrection*.
23. Jeunet, *Alien: Resurrection*.

inherent strangeness of the series until its shape is hardly recognizable. "From simple initial conditions cascades an unpredictable complexity," says Keller.[24] By transforming the *Alien* series from seriousness to farce, however briefly, *Alien: Resurrection* upends the story, complexifying it beyond the initial joke of its existence.

The first *Alien* hinted at a chaos lurking in the darkness between the stars by way of the alien, whose life cycle is unfathomable and unexpected. The next two sequels, for all their strengths, take the alien life cycle for granted, making it uniform through repetition, until the chaos is elided by predictability. Likewise, the inequality inherent in the series' social structures, particularly the inequality of the androids, is lost in the series' focus on Ripley's story only. By embracing the chaos inherent in *Alien*, and by satirizing its more serious themes, *Alien: Resurrection* sets the androids free, giving teeth and purpose to their existence, beyond existing just to serve. The androids are no longer tools but people, and like people they are volatile, emotional, unpredictable. The scientists attempt to control their situation, and it ends poorly for them. In the *Alien* universe, chaos always wins out over control; predictability cannot anticipate the unpredictable. Ripley and Call manage to survive because they are survivors, because they know that they cannot hope to control the alien; they know that their options are to either kill the alien, or to run, or else be killed themselves. The scientists do not understand this; instead, they try to control the uncontrollable, giving the alien queen a womb, splicing human DNA with that of the aliens, creating a skull-faced newborn alien that they hope to turn into their own self-propagating weapon.

Their attempts at control do them little good: the scientists are killed by their own test subjects, and Ripley

24. Keller, *Face of the Deep*, 39.

flushes the newborn out into the depths of space through a pinhole in the ship's hull. The newborn's grotesque, ordered body is returned to chaos as it is disassembled by the vacuum of space. The result is awe-inspiring and more than a little silly. Evil and exploitative systems in our own universe are rendered ridiculous by *Alien: Resurrection*, the entire series turned into a joke that refigures the place of the androids and their roles in the world of *Alien*, an un-flattening that affirms their personhood over the use and dismissal of androids in the first three films.[25]

Ripley and Call find themselves alone, flying low over an Earth neither of them expected to see. Call turns to Ripley as they break through the cloud cover, asking her what comes next.

"I don't know," replies Ripley. "I'm a stranger here myself."[26] Her strangeness stems from her status, not only as a human-alien hybrid, but also as a free person, free from the discreative influence of the alien race intertwined with her DNA, and free from the systems and militaries and companies who would use her abilities with no regard for her personhood. As Ripley and Call tear into Earth's atmosphere, they break away from their past lives: not crash-landing into the hard systems of use and discreation that have shaped their lives up until this point, but flying away into the possibility of a new life.

25. The alien life cycle, having been brought to its illogical conclusion, is left un-commented on, except for Ripley's choice to kill the newborn and so put an end to all human-alien hybrids that are not her.

26. Jeunet, *Alien: Resurrection*.

5

GOD DOESN'T BUILD
IN STRAIGHT LINES

Prometheus

Ripley and Call fly away to earth. Their story continues but we are no longer a part of it. We are left free to imagine myriad endings, branching and spiraling outward, each of them different, and each of them no longer the focus of the text. Instead, the *Alien* series follows a different path, a spiral inward and back away from the future, returning to the beginning of the story. *Prometheus* is a reset, placed in the same universe and preparing the scene for the events of the first *Alien*, less concerned with explaining *how* the events of *Alien* came to be and more preoccupied with understanding *why* they happened—with getting at the root cause of evil and suffering. *Alien* is imminent, almost-now and not-yet. The connective tissue between *Alien* and *Prometheus* is both apparent, in that they both take place within the same universe, and maddeningly unclear, in that the implied events between original and prequel are disconnected.

Prometheus marks the return of Ridley Scott to the series he began, and it marks the return of the series to its own origins—to the questions raised by the first film, then abandoned: Where did the alien come from? Where did the derelict spaceship come from, and what sort of civilization does it represent? In exploring these long-forgotten and un-answered questions, Scott folds in the questions that have permeated all of human existence as well: where did humanity come from? Who made us, and for what purpose? If we were purposefully made, where did evil and pain and death come from?

The only answers we receive from *Prometheus* are imprecise. They seed more questions instead of certainty—Ridley Scott himself stated that *Prometheus* would be "too neat, too clean"[1] if the connections between the two films were straight lines. Scott's attitude is one of comfort with complexity, a trait Keller would admire: just as Job and Genesis reexamine other origin stories that came before them, complicating rather than explaining their predecessors, so too does *Prometheus* dig at the roots of *Alien* before it. *Prometheus* does not seek to explain every piece of *Alien*'s absurd and terrifying mysteries; rather, it trains the story on the themes left in the shadows by the previous film's focus, seeking to poke at other mysteries instead of tying *Alien*'s central mystery off with a clean knot. *Prometheus* reaches for themes outside of its grasp rather than staying in familiar, comforting, shallow waters. There are no easy answers in the prequel film, only complications, but complication breeds the possibility of depth. *Prometheus* attempts to get at the root of evil actions,

1. Scott, *Prometheus*, director's commentary.

which stem from an attempt to exert control over chaos—by discreating other people, flattening them to tools and toys, and also by flattening the complexity of the cosmos, to stuff the universe down into an easily understandable box. As the scientists on the *Prometheus* mission discover, questions beget more questions; understanding of the universe reveals possibilities and potential, not concrete building blocks and easily explainable phenomena. It is chaos all the way down.

—

Keller and Scott each seek to re-examine texts taken for granted. Keller re-examines the first two verses of Genesis, finding the wonder in a passage often skimmed over. She roots this wonder in the voluminous masses of space, depths that recall the Big Bang and that might very well be a yawning chasm flecked with the floating lights of stars. "We gape back," Keller says, describing human reactions to the chasm of infinity. "We make marvelous machines for gaping."[2] She returns, again and again, to the depths of infinity that prefigure creation in Genesis. As with Keller's treatment of the creation story, *Prometheus* is a return to an inciting incident, often elided, at the beginning of *Alien:* the discovery of a derelict spacecraft, and of the fossilized skeleton with the gaping hole in its chest. The skeleton's existence is proof that humans are not alone in the universe, but, like the crew, *Alien's* focus passes over it, abandoning the dead body in the dark for a live organism that will leave more dead in its wake. The derelict, and its occupant, remain alone and forgotten in the universe until *Prometheus* picks up their pieces. The new story and the scientists who populate it occupy themselves with poking

2. Keller, *Face of the Deep,* xv.

into the holes left over from *Alien*, exploring how deep the gaping cavern inside the derelict goes. Their attempts to understand their world are fueled by wonder at the impossible bigness of the universe, and at the incredible coincidences that seem to indicate the creation of humanity by superior life forms. Unlike the scientists aboard the *Auriga*, the *Prometheus* scientists are not driven by a desire to capture the alien—they do not yet know of its existence, and they would be more interested in understanding the evolutionary biology of the alien more than its potential as a bioweapon anyway. Instead, their work is intended to unravel the mystery of their own creation, to explain the origins of life on Earth. Their motivations are good, but the approach is oversimplified, as though a single scientific discovery could solve the mystery of life so fully as to leave no room for doubt or complication, an echo of the ontological flattening brought on by the Fury–161 prisoners and their own simple religion. The *Prometheus* scientists seek simple, all-explaining answers, and in so doing they pave over the true complexity of the universe they live in.

Prometheus is an attempt to break free of the template established by previous *Alien* films.[3] The beckoning signal of the original movies becomes a historical artifact, a cave painting repeated across ancient human cultures who would have had no contact with each other. The repeated painting depicts a giant being pointing to the stars: not sound waves bouncing across time and space, but a static image, a physical thing that can be photographed and studied. The scientists who discover the cave paintings interpret them as an invitation, believing that the giant being pointing to the stars is an alien intelligence, the creator and shaper of human life. They call the giants *Engineers*, and they hope to find them someday.

3. Sobchack, "Between a Rock and a Hard Place," 32.

These scientists are not truckers, nor prisoners, nor military personnel; they pursue their work voluntarily rather than being coerced by the company employing them. They are funded as a scientific mission by the Weyland Corporation. (The "-Yutani" merger has not yet occurred, and the Company has not yet become a faceless bureaucratic conglomeration.) It is a tech company, pouring wealth into the pockets of its aging founder, Peter Weyland, who in turn funds scientific missions like the quest for the Engineers. Weyland's biggest scientific breakthrough is the creation of lifelike androids who can empathize with the humans who surround them. The current model, David, tends the scientific vessel *Prometheus* as it voyages across the galaxy toward the star formation depicted in the scientists' cave painting. Both the painting and the star system lie in darkness until they are discovered: one in a rocky outcropping on earth, the other in the depths of space. They are both too similar to be coincidental, separated as they are by the expanse of space and time: an indication of Keller's "fluctuations" and "repetitions" in the nonlinear universe.[4] Patterns repeat themselves as the scientists circle around guesses and theories and attempts at explanations of their own origins, getting closer to their origins with every step, but never reaching a comprehensive understanding of anything they see.

———

As mentioned in the first chapter, *Alien* begins in medias res, the wheels of the plot already in motion. The creature on the derelict ship was dead long years before the *Nostromo*'s journey; the Company's orders were sent days before the *Nostromo* started its return trip, before Ash

4. Keller, *Face of the Deep*, 189.

joined the crew. *Alien* is a film in the process of becoming itself; the only catalyst it needs to begin its story is the distress beacon from LV–426 that wakes up the crew. The films that follow unfold in fractal patterns outward from the inciting incident of Kane's death, iterations and re-iterations on the same theme in different flavors and tones, what Keller would call feedback loops through time.[5] They are revisions of the original story, telling a tale of horror and escape over and over, each one revealing new aspects of evil at work in the universe, whether they are previously unknown abilities of the alien creature, or new revelations of systems of abuse.

These examples of evil are always evolutions of an already-familiar theme, informed by what has come before them, and making their predecessors more complicated and more sinister once considered with the whole of the story. The lone alien is one of many, and the Company's exploitation of others is systematic (*Aliens*); the alien can prey on animals just as well as human beings, and the Company's exploitation is spiritual and existential, not just economical (*Alien3*); the alien can be spliced with human DNA and body parts, and the Company's established patterns of abuse and discreation will metastasize into whatever organization comes after them (*Alien: Resurrection*).

These evolutions never clarify the alien's origins or bloodlust, nor do they demonstrate the decisions the Company made that allowed them to start down the path of treating life as cheap. The first four films, for all their complexity, elide the beginning of the story. They turn a blind eye to the chaos of space, focusing on a single human, trading uncertainty and mystery for variations on the same theme as Ripley escapes from and returns to danger. The text of the first four films of the *Alien* series focuses

5. Keller, *Face of the Deep*, 189.

on the personal journey of a single character, which, when viewed through Keller's lens, reveals the vastness of a large and uncaring universe.

Keller confronts the human tendency to shy away from the impersonal magnitude of the cosmos. We choose instead to focus on more granular problems set in "the human scale of need,"[6] she says, but if we pay attention we will be overwhelmed by the complexity of each individual story the world confronts us with, grains of sand that pile up into a "chaos of suffering"[7] in a world that seems broken and incomplete. It is our fearful retreat from the scale of space that forces us to acknowledge the boundless depths of infinity, even as we turn away from it. In our fear, we shun the chaotic depths and darkness as bad, as nothing, as worthless, choosing instead to deal in finite absolutes that we can conceive of and attempt to explain. Keller's *Face of the Deep* is a refiguring of our relationship to that which can never be explained or controlled, a return to the source and the beginning of time. In returning, Keller posits that the unknown chaos at the beginning of the world is something to be appreciated, even though it cannot be conquered or fully understood.[8]

Prometheus follows this same line of thought: confronting the frightening black depths inside the derelict, contemplating the origin of the alien, and by extension the origins of humanity. It is less an attempt to explain that which has been left unexplained than it is a recombining of the lore of the previous *Alien* films with Greek mythology. There are no one-to-one correlations between *Alien* and *Prometheus*, although there are similarities between the two. *Prometheus* does not set out to give easy answers to

6. Keller, *Face of the Deep,* xv.

7. Keller, *Face of the Deep,* xvi.

8. Keller, *Face of the Deep,* 105.

the questions about *how* the events of *Alien* were set up, but instead contemplates the reasons *why* the universe of *Alien* came to exist in the first place. It goes about this by showing a team of human scientists as they themselves attempt—and fail—to distill the origins of the universe into an explanation they can easily understand.

Prometheus opens with an eclipse as day breaks over the face of a planet, light breaking over darkness like a tidal wave.[9] Then in a rush come clouds, steam rising from the rocks, snow, glaciers, lakes, rivers—everywhere water, or at least the signs that water has passed through, carving canyons and scoring moraines across the planet's rocky face. There are no signs of life, except one. The curved shield of a ship hovers over a waterfall,[10] then turns and slips into the atmosphere, alien in its smooth shape. A hooded figure with black eyes and skin like marble, left behind on the planet, uncovers a cup of something that begins to corrode when it makes contact with the air. The figure drinks it without hesitating, and its skin begins to split and scar, the drink carving black canyons into the figure's body just as the water carved rivers into the landscape. Somewhere deep inside its body, DNA withers and splits. Outside, the figure falls apart, its bones snapping as it tumbles down a waterfall. It disintegrates into black dust, and as the water pounds down upon the remains, its DNA recombines, twisting back into shape, cells turning red with oxygen, pumping with life to the heartbeat of the waterfall. Life has been seeded into the face of the chaotic waters: a creation story, complete with

9. The shot is nearly an exact replica of the opening of *2001: A Space Odyssey*, albeit shorter. Kubrick's work was the first science fiction that Ridley Scott respected, and he modeled the realism of Alien on *2001*. Rinzler, *Making of Alien*, 14.

10 "Now the earth was formless and empty, darkness was over the surface of the deep, and the Spirit of God was hovering over the waters." Gen 1:2.

Keller's *tehomic* deeps and chaos "self-organizing" back into a "genesis of order."[11] There is no explanation of why the figure killed itself to create more life, why this planet was chosen, if there are more planets seeded by men with marble skin, and if so, how many. Their purposes in creating life remain opaque, their intentions unclear; we are left to wonder why they chose to seed life when and where they did, on a planet that already existed.[12] The consequences of their choice to create life where they did will reverberate[13] across time and space, no more controllable than the onslaught of the waterfall that carried the DNA to its new home in the universe.

This prologue scene sets the stage for the film to follow: a watery planet floating in deep space, with the awful grandeur of immense cliffs and tumbling water priming the audience to consider the majesty of the world in all its chaotic detail. *Prometheus* trades the yellowy shades of its predecessors for a darker grade, a return to the grays and blues of *Alien* and *Aliens*, but this time tinted with the lush green of life. Water is everywhere, slick and damp and cold: this is a primordial swamp, a petri dish, a cradle of life. The reedy theme of *Alien* is exchanged for horns, in keeping with the majesty of the cliffs and waterways of the film's first few minutes. *Prometheus* is not a small-scale story about a crew of human beings, but a fable about the origins of humanity, transplanted just a few short years into the future.

This future threads its way back roundabout to the in medias res of *Alien* by way of small details and nods

11. Keller, *Face of the Deep*, 188.

12. The chaotic waters of the planet—in his interviews and film commentary, Ridley Scott bristled at the idea that the planet must be Earth, saying instead that it is a planet very much *like* Earth—map closely to the face of the waters, already in existence, from Gen 1:1–2.

13. Or, in Keller's words, "fluctuate." Keller, *Face of the Deep*, 189.

to previous films. The titular ship *Prometheus*, by design, harks back to the *Nostromo*, a ship that does not yet exist in the film's timeline. Both vessels share cryopods and escape modules not designed to take the entire crew. Both have octagonal doorways and low ceilings, bridges lit by thousands of tiny lights and angular control panels tangled in wires and switches. A dippy bird drinks from a cup; the warning *X*'s that strobe across the bridge computer displays echo the *X*'s from the *Nostromo's* own self-destruct message. The *Prometheus*, like the *Nostromo* before it, travels to a system populated with volcanically rocky planetoids covered in inhospitable atmospheres. But the cycle back to the origins of the alien, and of the derelict, is an open-ended circle. The events of *Prometheus* do not take place on LV–426, but on LV–223. The origins of *Alien* within the story of *Prometheus* are imprecise, imperfect, inexact; we can never fully understand them, and attempts to explain them would be inaccurate.

—

In *Face of the Deep*, Keller lays out a framework for approaches to understanding and knowledge: it is vital to understand *how* and *why* human beings go about the business of study, their approaches and the effects of their understanding. She first describes Western understanding as possessive and domineering; a need to build on the knowledge of one's predecessors, to take it over, to appropriate it, to own knowledge—and the thing understood—more fully than its creator ever could.[14] This model of understanding is focused on completeness, but it engenders possession and colonization: to truly understand something is to know it better than any other, to have

14. Keller, *Face of the Deep*, 105.

a grasp on a singular, concrete truth from an objective standpoint. This concrete vision of knowledge is ambitious and impossible. No human being can hold the map of molecules needed to form another person inside their head, let alone understand why that person does the things they do or behaves the way they do or makes the choices they choose to make. This knowledge is rooted in control, both colonialist and patriarchal, an ontology that fixes moments in time and freezes their growth and development, trapping them forever in the mind of the person who understands them.[15]

Up until *Prometheus*, the *Alien* films present a universe that can be interpreted simply and easily. Space is cold, Weyland-Yutani is colder, and everywhere there are monsters. Evil exploits, and good fights back against exploitation. The plot is linear. Rather than continuing in a linear progression, *Prometheus* complicates the universe of *Alien*. As Keller returns again and again to Genesis's inciting incident and its "nonlinear" effects on creation, *Prometheus* returns to the beginning of the story, diving into darkness long left behind.[16] It also presents characters whose methods of understanding are grasping and exploitative, despite their best intentions.

Holloway and Shaw, the two scientists who discovered the cave paintings, lead the *Prometheus* mission. They want nothing more than to talk to the Engineers who made human beings, to "meet their makers."[17] They want to know the objective truth about creation, to map

15. On the other end of the spectrum lies poststructuralist interpretation, an attempt at understanding that, Keller says, "posit[s] the text as an incommensurable alien," something that can be grasped at, but never fully understood (Keller, *Face of the Deep*, 105).

16. Keller, *Face of the Deep*, 186–89.

17. Scott, *Prometheus*.

it, to explore it, to study it, to understand it. In so doing, they hope to understand the origins of humanity, and to unlock the secrets of life: its beginning, its continuation, and its end. Their intentions are not bad; there is nothing wrong with wanting to understand the universe. But their search for a single answer elides the complexity of the universe, flattening their world only into the dimensions they can see. The result is unintended exploitation and misunderstanding, which leads to calcified patterns of use and ongoing exploitation, painful consequences that will reverberate across the centuries and into the *Alien* films that were released before *Prometheus*, but that come after its events on a linear timeline.

Weyland funded the *Prometheus* mission because he himself wanted to meet the Engineers and ask them to extend his own life; he considers the scientific mission to be a cover for his own purposes, Holloway and Shaw and their team pawns in his quest to defeat mortality. Holloway is left disillusioned when the *Prometheus* mission reaches their destination and finds the Engineers dead, wiped out by some catastrophe thousands of years before. He expects to find living beings, not dead bodies, an apparent dead end for his own journey of understanding because the only answers he hoped to find were possessed by people long gone. His single-perspective view affects the rest of the team. When they find the Engineer bodies, the geologist leaves, unnerved by the sudden knowledge that there is life in the universe that is other than human, and unable to acknowledge the importance of viewpoints beyond the bounds of his narrow scientific focus. He says that he signed up to study rocks, not corpses.[18] Likewise, the biologist loses his own life to a snakelike alien, overconfident that his experience with terrestrial animals will carry him through

18. Scott, *Prometheus*.

a close encounter. Shaw's attempts to understand the end of the Engineers become possessive and exploitative. She risks the safety of the team to retrieve an Engineer head for study, and tries to trick the preserved brain into thinking it is still alive by charging it with an electrical current. The re-animation experiment proves painful for the Engineer head, until it can no longer take the stress; it explodes, leaving the scientists with a discreated mass of tissue. Shaw manages to isolate the Engineer's DNA from the mess, using it to prove her theory that human beings came from the Engineers, but the answers she gets from the DNA are still one-dimensional. She is still no closer to understanding why the Engineers seeded the Earth with life, let alone how they went about it. None of the scientists are capable of seeing beyond their own disciplines to the big picture.

In contrast to possessive and one-dimensional models of knowledge, Keller proposes a "*tehomic* hermeneutic," an interpretive framework that eschews singular truths and definite answers, "one that has given up the straight path for an endless labyrinth of interpretation."[19] Singular *yes!* understanding and ownership of knowledge is traded for plurality of perspective. In return, the chaotic world is no longer subjected to ownership, nor left to its own devices, but is opened into a space for different understandings, according to the standpoint and perspective of the people doing the interpreting, and unbounded by linear time.[20] This plurality risks chaos and contradiction, but it also allows for depth perception not afforded by a singular viewpoint.[21] Rather than flattening knowledge of creation (and by extension, the Creator) to one dominant perspective, Keller argues for multiple viewpoints, multiple perspectives, a

19. Keller, *Face of the Deep*, 104.
20. Keller, *Face of the Deep*, 189.
21. Keller, *Face of the Deep*, 5.

wealth of variety and a richer image of God and the universe that God made. Human beings are afforded glimpses of this complexity, made richer by a multiplicity of perspectives, but, as in the story of Job, God withholds some of the information. Domination seeks to tame complexity, to boil the wonder out of it.

As the *Prometheus* mission breaks atmosphere on LV–223, they find an Engineer road leading to a pyramid. Holloway points the road out first, saying, "God doesn't build in straight lines."[22] The universe is part of a vast, chaotic creation, dense and ultimately unfathomable. Human beings can try to map it and subdue it, but they will never fully understand it, and their attempts to impose their understanding in it stand in stark contrast to the vast chaos that remains. Their knowledge is a small, straight line amongst a tumble of giant mountains, a scar on the landscape that scratches the surface, but that cannot hope to envelop the entirety of the world around it. Any attempt to impose one's own will on the chaos, to exploit it and to unmake it, to reduce it to simple linear cause and effect, would be folly.

—

For all their attempts to grasp creation outside of their immediate experience, the humans on the *Prometheus* mission have a difficult time recognizing the effects of their decisions to create. David, despite being an early model of android, a predecessor to Ash, Bishop, and Call, is far more complicated and alive than the human beings around him give him credit for. Like the androids in the other *Alien* films before him, David functions as an extension of the ship. He is another pair of hands, a monitor to ensure

22. Scott, *Prometheus*.

the *Prometheus* functions on its long voyage, an aid, a servant, a porter, a bartender, a translator. When David asks Holloway why he thinks humans made him, Holloway responds, "We made you 'cos we could."[23] When David tells him how disappointing that must feel to hear such a reason from one's creator, drawing a parallel between Holloway's disillusionment and his own, Holloway laughs. He denies the possibility that David could have any feelings. David's fingerprints bear the Weyland logo: he is the Company's creation and their property. Weyland himself refers to David as the closest thing to a son he will ever have, while in the same breath dismissing the possibility that David might have a soul. To Weyland, David is an intelligent tool, a robot, an achievement—more valuable an achievement than Weyland's own daughter—but not an independent being, and certainly not a person.

But personhood is something that David has. He behaves similarly to the human beings he was designed to imitate, even when he is alone; he watches *Lawrence of Arabia* on the long voyage, dying his hair to match Peter O'Toole's T. E. Lawrence and modeling himself after the character. He combs his hair, buttons himself up, repeats Lawrence's lines to himself in strict cadence, not because he is a robot, but because, like O'Toole's Lawrence, the careful exterior hides an unpredictable interior, chaotic and grandiose.[24] Despite the attitudes of the human beings

23. Scott, *Prometheus*. "Because we could" is a blunt tautology, blind creation in a vacuum for the sake of the act of making, with no regard to the consequences caroming off the act, either for good or for evil. It elides the responsibility the creators have for what comes next.

24. In *Alien3*, Ripley was modeled on Joan of Arc, but her similarities with the character are unselfconscious: Ripley is not modeling herself after Joan, because she does not see herself as a martyr. David feels kinship with Lawrence, a closeted gay

who created and surround him, David has developed his own personhood. Unlike the humans who search for their origins among the stars, David understands his own creators perfectly well, watching their dreams as they hibernate through their journey to LV–223, questioning the wisdom of their motivations to create and to seek their own creators when his own are so flawed and so disappointing. David's own actions and motivations remain slippery; it is unclear if his every move has been dictated by Weyland, or if he chooses to act of his own free will. He discovers an Engineer ship, and a stockpile of Engineer bioweapons in stacks and rows of amphora, while exploring alone and unsupervised. It is left unclear whether Weyland told David to conduct his own experiments with the bioweapons, or if David chose to do so of his own volition. David is rendered unknowable by his opaque motivations, a creation that has taken on a life of its own.

David's inner life becomes apparent with his discovery of the Engineer ship. Once on the bridge, he triggers a security recording of the Engineers who had once piloted the ship. Their ghostly forms, going about their business, affect the functions of the ship, tripping its power supply and activating a star map. The map blossoms across the inside of the bridge, filling it with countless cold blue lights, each one representing a star or a system. As the holographic Engineer at the helm flips through the map, David stands

---

Englishman who finds himself for a time in Arabia, because the two mask their hidden, true identities beneath a placid exterior. Like Lawrence, David's calm, robotic demeanor hides a violently chaotic consciousness. Lawrence cannot be himself, nor attain greatness, until he leaves the suffocating confines of English society. David believes that he, too, is destined for greatness: he is the "son" of Peter Weyland, and one of the first androids capable of passing for human, and he cannot realize his potential until he leaves his planet of origin and finds himself in the chaotic wilds of space.

at its center, a smile spreading across his face, arms raised while he spins around, enveloped by the stars. The score's horns swell: David is not simply gathering information, nor is he coldly calculating his next move. He is filled with wonder and delight, dwarfed by the stars spinning around him in recreation of the geocentric model of the universe. He reaches upward, childlike, for a planet floating above him, then cradles it in his hands, pondering its surface as it spins in place. The planet is Earth, and as he holds it, David's position from moments before as a small being among the cosmos is changed to that of a giant holding a globe, the planet that produced him now small and fragile within his grasp. The child of Earth's children, underestimated and dismissed by his own creators, has realized his own potential. Weyland's assertion that David can have no soul is a dismissal of David's inherent worth as a created being, a statement that places him on a tier lower than the human beings he serves, subjecting him to their control.

—

By the end of *Prometheus*, all attempts to control, to dominate, and to possess are thwarted. Weyland's life is ended by the very Engineer he hoped would extend his life; he is killed in his attempt to cheat death. The scientists never learn why or how the Engineers created humanity. David's attempt to speak with the surviving Engineers is met with violence, and the Engineers seem set on returning to the planet to destroy their own work. They too are thwarted, killed in a collision between their ship and the *Prometheus*. The last living Engineer is attacked by one of his own bio-weapons, a monstrous proto-facehugger, one of the lone acknowledgments that *Prometheus* takes place in the same universe as *Alien*. The end of the film is explosive, but small, surprising in its unsatisfying nature. There are no definite answers, no reasons given for the actions on the screen. The only answer *Prometheus* can give us is that there is chaos out among the stars, and while we are produced by it, we cannot control it; attempting to grasp for complete understanding is to simplify the answer such that it will always somehow disappoint.

Prometheus ends with Shaw, injured and alone, with no answers to her questions and precious little hope. All she has is David, an Engineer ship, and a burning desire to understand why the Engineers would want to create human life and then choose to destroy it. She has abandoned her need to know how the Engineers made life; she knows that she may never know. Her theories were reductive pictures, imperfect views of a system too complex for her to capture and to understand; her attempts to explain everything so definitively were attempts to wrap her arms around a massive universe. She thought she knew what she would find; she admits that she was wrong.

Shaw takes David and the remaining Engineer ship, leaving LV–233 behind. "There is only death here,"[25] she says. She is speaking about the literal planet, but through Keller's lens, she could also be describing attempts to bring the *Prometheus* story into a linear, bounded, limited understanding, which denies the possibilities of complexity and attempts to deconstruct creation into a simplified viewpoint. But it is New Year's Day, and a new beginning, the start of a new journey. Shaw will not return to Earth; she is "still searching,"[26] she says, and she pilots the ship away into the atmosphere, in search of a new source of knowledge.

25. Scott, *Prometheus*.
26. Scott, *Prometheus*.

6

NOTHING BESIDE REMAINS

Alien: Covenant

S haw flies away from LV–223, her ship's path curving slightly as it breaks atmosphere. Like her flight, the line from *Prometheus* to *Alien: Covenant* is nearly straight. More than any other *Alien* film, *Alien: Covenant* is a direct sequel to its predecessor, alike in interests and in appearance. But *Alien: Covenant* is also part of a looping path. It is a re-figuring of *Prometheus's* more opaque themes and a clarification of David's motivations and desires. It serves to distill all five preceding *Alien* films into a single story, self-contained and standalone, a summation of all that has come before it.

Alien: Covenant rolls up all previous *Alien* movies' themes—terror, isolation, the feeling of being exploited, and the questions and actions that those feelings engender— and distills them into one story. Like the first *Alien*, it has a limited cast and an eerie affect, with its tiny crew exploring the long-dead ruins of a once-civilized planet and finding those ruins haunted. Like *Aliens*, it punctuates its story with bursts of surprising action: a rough landing in a drop ship, an explosion that leaves the crew stranded on an unfamiliar planet, the rattle of automatic gunfire. Like *Alien3*, the crash brings the stranded survivors into contact with longtime residents of the planet, one whose very personhood had been negated by the Company: as with the prisoners on Fury–161 in *Alien3*, so with the android David in *Alien: Covenant*. Like *Alien: Resurrection*, *Alien: Covenant* is primarily interested in the personhood of its android characters: the aliens themselves are treated as frightening for the first time since *Alien3*, but they are relegated to secondary players in deference to David's story. Like its immediate predecessor *Prometheus*, *Alien: Covenant* is ambitious. It is a thrill ride, a philosophical enquiry, and another stepping stone between prequel and original film. *Alien: Covenant* is the sinew that ties all six *Alien* films into a cohesive whole. It is a shorthand for its predecessors, a distillation of the stories presented by all the other *Alien* movies that came before it, all without negating the mystery of the origins of the alien creatures. It also serves to sum up the themes of each of the *Alien* films before it.

—

Alien: Covenant* coheres visually with *Prometheus*. Both films share the same blue-green color palette. Both indulge in sweeping landscape shots, floating high above mountains, tracing the flow of water from cloud to river to lake, dripping with moisture and with the potential for life. *Alien: Covenant*'s set design recalls the first *Alien* as well, just as *Prometheus* did. The ship *Covenant*'s bridge, like that of the *Prometheus*, is boxy and festooned with wires; both are based on the design for the *Nostromo*. The *Covenant's* computer has a feminine voice, unlike the masculine voices of the *Auriga* and the *Prometheus*, and the crew of the *Covenant* addresses their computer as "Mother." Their EVA suits are boxy, like the suits worn by the *Nostromo's* crew, and when the *Covenant's* displays show a warning signal, they flash in *X*'s that recall both the collision alert of the *Prometheus* and the self-destruct message of the *Nostromo*.

The *Covenant's* bridge has its own dippy bird, forever drinking from a cup of water, a knickknack reminder of the *Alien* series' cyclical structure. Like the bird, *Alien's* ⌐over⌐ characters (and viewers) return to the same source over and over, repeating the events that came before, forever compelled to drink without fully slaking their thirst. Evil enacts a cycle of use and abuse, a motivation to discreate and toolify other beings; the characters in the *Alien* films confront the same societal ills again and again, each time in slightly different forms.[1] We try to progress past the sins of our ancestors but find ourselves facing the same problems, fractal iterations of original sin.[2] Likewise, the audience returns over and over to the same *Alien* films, expecting to see the same things they've seen before, elated when familiar touchstones like the dippy bird and the facehugger appear, and yet disappointed when the film is too much like its predecessors. The cyclical nature of *Alien* films should not be surprising. Its repetition is an inherent part of its structure, not a flaw.[3] The series' repetitions do not dull its ideas over time; they draw them out, allowing old ideas to be clarified and refined.

---

1. The alien's design—and the designs of the facehuggers and chestbursters—varies with each film.

2. Keller, *Face of the Deep*, 80.

3. Zoller Seitz, "Alien: Covenant."

Though it shares *Prometheus*'s color palette, *Alien: Covenant* is lit in chiaroscuro like a Goya painting, deep shadows causing its pale subjects to stand out against the black. A cloaked figure, backlit by a flare, stands tall in the gloom of a wheat field after dark; a row of cypress trees grows in orderly lines against the curved dome of an ancient building; an alien crouches over its victim, its elbows and knees sticking out spider-like from its body, bone-white and almost glowing within the depths of a cave. The effect throws the subjects of the film into relief, allowing each character to stand out against the gloomy backdrop. The result is an emphasis on the individual, and not on the abstract themes that threatened to swallow *Prometheus*. *Alien: Covenant* layers on a touch of the Romantic to the entire *Alien* series, and in so doing, it transforms the story from a human struggle against the external chaos of nature into a human struggle against the ingrained, internal fear of that unknown chaos, and against the systematic evil that springs from fear of the unknown. This struggle is apparent in three of *Alien: Covenant*'s main characters: two humans, one android.

—

The human characters of *Alien: Covenant* take on shades of their predecessors from the series, attempting to get at the traits that made those original characters tick. Daniels's character closely parallels those of Ripley and Hicks, while Oram resembles Gorman and Andrews. The security team on board the Covenant make up a private citizen version of the Colonial Marines, albeit with less outward bravado; to them their occupation is less a calling than a job, a role to play as the crew of the Covenant transports their cargo of colonists and terraforming equipment to their new lives on a distant planet.[4] The entire crew is made of couples, ensuring that each person is in a relationship with at least one other on board, that no one person should be left alone.

Oram, the *Covenant*'s de facto captain, follows in Gorman's and Andrews' footsteps from *Aliens* and *Alien3*. He takes command of the ship after the captain dies unexpectedly, victim of a fire on board set off by a neutrino burst. His approach to leadership is the same as Ripley's from the first *Alien*: wedded to protocols and preparation, a desire to control all possible outcomes. As with Ripley's protocols and boundaries on board the Nostromo, Oram's preparation is not an inherently bad thing; preparation and hard work will benefit the crew as they begin their new lives on a strange planet. But Oram fails to account for the needs of the individuals under his command. He asserts his knowledge—that of the protocol book—over the plurality of experiences of the crew under his care. He brushes past their need to mourn, to process, and to understand, insisting that they flatten their reactions to the unexpected and bottle their emotions as they fix the damage to their ship. He brushes over their reactions of shock and fear and sadness, expecting them to behave exactly as their onboard android, Walter: all rationale, no individuality. Oram is uncertain in his leadership role and demanding of his crew, unable to lead without a heavy touch. He refuses the crew their request to have a funeral for their lost captain and crewmates. Like Andrews, he claims authority that he has been handed, but has not earned; like Gorman, he tries to control the uncontrollable.

4. Unlike its predecessors, *Alien: Covenant* does not interrogate the colonialism inherent in terraforming. *Aliens* covered those bases already, and *Alien: Covenant* has moved on to exploring the relationship between creator and created.

Daniels—the wife of the *Covenant's* dead captain, and Oram's second-in-command—is much more suited for leadership than Oram because of her ability to adapt. She is flexible where Oram is rigid, but solid where he is inadequate. When the rest of the crew is still shell-shocked from the fire, she goes about her duties, securing the terraforming equipment in the docking bay, then burying her husband in the funeral that Oram had forbidden. Daniels is more cautious than her late husband, who used to free climb mountains, and who wanted to go on the mission because it would be an adventure, an opportunity to explore a wild new planet. She followed him and his desire to build a log cabin on a lake on a brand new world; she had never intended to be alone out amongst the stars. She admits to Walter that she does not know what she is doing on the *Covenant*, that she has no idea what to do with the nails in the hold. But she does not fold under the pressure of her grief, nor does she back down.

Nor does she attempt to control the chaotic circumstances that descend upon them shortly after they land on the planet. When two of their security team become rapidly sick, Daniels is one of the few landing party members to remain calm, to keep a steady head when the infected men convulse and die, their bodies split by pale white aliens who then proceed to hunt the rest of the crew. Like Ripley and Hicks before her, she adapts to her environment, improvising where she needs to, running when she cannot. She is not in control, and she knows it, and she chooses not to fight it. She hardly blinks when David appears, a hooded specter on an uninhabited planet. He ushers the few surviving crew to his base, a stronghold built for giants, populated by blackened statues of the dead. The crew are left trapped on the planet, with no lander and no hope of returning to the *Covenant* through a gathering ion storm above them.

———

The David that the *Covenant* crew finds alone in the wild is the same David from the *Prometheus* mission years before. He tells them that the planet they are on was once home to the Engineers. David and Shaw found it through Shaw's search for answers. David released the Engineers' bioweapons upon arrival, the amphora deploying from their ship in the shape of a DNA spiral before raining clouds of death upon the planet's residents. The bioweapons have the potential for both life and death.

David is a Frankenstein figure, both monster and scientist, a being who was created then exploited as a tool who turned around and exploited others in his attempt to create new life, perpetuating the cycle of discreation and exploitation.

Like Frankenstein's monster, David was created by Weyland in pursuit of scientific discovery. Within moments of his inception, he walks, names himself, plays the piano, and questions his maker about his purpose in the world, moving from simple words and movements to complex art and reasoning within a matter of seconds. Weyland calls David perfect—a tribute to his own creative ability, and not a judgment of David's own worth. Weyland calls himself David's father, a title more personal and intimate than that of *creator*, but he treats David as a by-product of his own genius and creativity: a tool, a toy, someone whose questions can be dismissed. He refuses to think that humans could be a "random by-product of molecular circumstance,"[5] both an affirmation of the possibility that human beings could have been created by some intelligent being, and a rejection

5. Scott, *Alien: Covenant.*

of the chaos that predates the ordered world.[6] When David reminds Weyland of his mortality, Weyland forces him to cross the room and serve him. David acquiesces, walking barefoot across the room to pour his creator a cup of tea. He is interrupted by a cut to a shot of stars and a blink of light, a ship small against the scale of the cosmos, speeding across the frame. The cut traps David in a posture of servitude that he was created for and has no say in, forever holding out a teacup for Weyland to take. David is left discreated, a tool and not a person; like Frankenstein's monster, created to be more than human, then abandoned for being too inhuman.

David's rejection as a tool by his creator leads him to abandon his creator in turn; after Weyland is killed by an Engineer at the end of *Prometheus*, David leaves LV–223 with Shaw, not because he wants to understand why the Engineers wanted to destroy humanity, but because he is curious about the Engineers' bioweapons. A tool himself, he sees their potential as discreative tools. After David and Shaw land on the Engineer planet, the inhabitants wiped out by David's arsenal, David sets himself to unlocking new applications for his remaining weapons. He is uninterested in creating a companion for himself; like Weyland before him, David prefers a position of power over others, a vantage point from which he can leverage his control. Like Frankenstein's monster, he models himself on John Milton's Lucifer, preferring to reign in the hell of the Engineer planet over serving in the heaven of human exploration. David embraces his role as a demon, taking on the mantle of Frankenstein-as-scientist. He experiments on Shaw and on the wildlife on the planet, merging them together with pieces of the Engineer's bioweapons, until he bioengineers organisms that closely resemble the alien that first stalked the crew of the *Nostromo* and looses them on the stranded

6. Keller, *Face of the Deep*, 60.

crew of the *Covenant*. Because David's desire to create, like Weyland's, stems from a desire and a need to control, all David can do is to discreate. Rather than allowing the creatures on the Engineer planet to flourish, he snuffs them out, splicing them together into little monsters of his own, until he manages to create a creature that grows inside an egg, that springs out and grasps at a host's face in order to lay its young inside the host's chest, until the young bursts out and becomes a killing machine. David, who had been called a "perfect"[7] creation by Weyland, then denied his personhood by his own creator, creates his own "perfect organism"[8]—his words, an echo of Ash who will come after him—that will go on to discreate and destroy every human being it sees.

David does not see his acts of creation as an evil; he believes that he is achieving perfection by following in the footsteps of his father-creator. He desires nothing more than to create something magnificent, cultivating an image after the Romantic poets, quoting Shelley's Ozymandias as he shows Walter his laboratory: "Look on my works, ye mighty, and despair."[9]

Crucially, like Frankenstein's monster, and like the Ozymandias of the poem, David's model is the last of his kind. He is succeeded by Walter, an android who is technologically more advanced, but who has had the passion programmed out of him. Walter cannot emote like David can; his feelings have been dialed back, David's clipped English accent traded for Walter's blunt Midwestern one. Walter, unlike David, has been prohibited from creating anything of his own. David teaches Walter how to play the flute, but Walter will never be able to produce the same

7. Scott, *Alien: Covenant*.

8. Scott, *Alien: Covenant* and Scott, *Alien*.

9. Shelley, *Ozymandias*.

melodies that David does. Walter operates out of a sense of duty, an understanding that he is a servant, created to be a tool, and nothing more; David's notions of free will and of greatness are stamped out of the updated model,[10] a retraction of the personhood that had once been granted to his technological ancestor.

When David quotes *Ozymandias*, he leaves off the last few lines and misattributes the poem to Byron. Walter corrects him, completing the poem:

> "Nothing beside remains. Round the decay
> Of that colossal Wreck, boundless and bare,
> The lone and level sands stretch far away."[11]

To change the world into one's own image, to force all others into submission until they have no hope of agency, is to deny their personhood. *Ozymandias* begins by painting a portrait of a king who takes complete control of his kingdom and exerts command over his subjects, but who too must die; after his death, his kingdom is reclaimed by the desert, swallowed by the chaos that he tried to hold off through force of his own charisma.

—

Alien: Covenant is a reckoning between David and the humans who created him, then denied his personhood; it is also a reckoning between human beings and the chaotic potential they find in the depths of space. Walter refers to the neutrino burst that damaged the *Covenant* as a "random

---

10. The Covenant crew treats Walter just as all other *Alien* characters have treated androids: as a second set of hands, as a tool, someone else at whom to bark orders.

11. Shelley, *Ozymandias*.

localized event,"[12] something that could have happened anywhere, with no warning or way to detect it, a result of the chaotic deeps of space doing whatever it is the chaotic deeps of space will do as they oscillate in and out of order.[13] It is neither good nor bad, it just *is*. Humanity has no way to prevent such bursts, or to prepare for them; the bursts simply happen. The unknown is not bad, but Keller describes them as frightening, something human beings shy away from or attempt to control, and in their controlling, deny the complexity of the world that is, trading it for an incomplete image. The humans of the *Covenant*, in their attempts to control chaos, run up against consequences in the form of David, who twists the chaotic potential of the depths into a monster far worse than the depths of unknown potential. David's efforts end in discreation, solidifying a pattern of fear and use into something that humanity cannot face, cannot escape, and cannot control.

The androids are the key to the entire *Alien* series. They reveal much about the attitude of human beings toward others not like them. Ash and Bishop and Walter are tools; David and Call are unnerving precisely because they do not behave like the tools the humans around them expect them to be. They are creations of humanity, and they are sentient creatures themselves, regardless of their intended function, and in spite of the way that they are treated. David's volatile creativity is a source of chaotic potential, but once Weyland treats that potential as a tool, David's personhood is left corrupted. Weyland's rejection of his "son" at the beginning of the film becomes an act of original sin, a simple act that will reverberate across time and space to the harm of all other beings who come into contact with an android in David's line. To be an android in the *Alien* series is to be

12. Scott, *Alien: Covenant*.
13. Keller, *Face of the Deep*, 189.

subjected to alienation and domination—to be infected by Keller's understanding of sin; the relation of this sin is cyclical, trapping all who follow within the cycle of sin and use, domination and discreation.[14]

The androids are each created in and subjected to the same original sin of Weyland and David. Ash is a calcified descendant of David and Walter, creative when he needs to be, staid everywhere else; in all he does he is contemptuous of the humans who created him, pitiless and mocking. He enables the Company to use the crew of the *Nostromo* as bait in their bid to capture the alien on LV–426. Bishop, unlike Ash, is a more compliant tool, more apparently affable, with a hint of an agreeable personality. He does not bring harm to the humans around him, but he is still used and almost happy to be used by his human companions. Call, though she was created by other androids and not by human beings as a response to the cycle of human use and abuse, is still treated as a tool by the human beings who surround her. She was an unsuccessful attempt to break the cycle of toolification, another unwilling participant in the cycle, damaged by her own creators. She is left with guilt and shame for her state of being, which she had no choice but to partake in.

—

Utter control denies the freedoms—and by extension, the personhood—of others. It engenders the desire to use others as tools, to discreate them down to their most basic parts, and to use those parts as pieces in one's own creations. Control, which despite the illusion that control could affect the outcome of a given situation, leads to a flattening of others, a denial of the plurality of experience, a preference

14. Keller, *Face of the Deep*, 80.

for one hegemonic viewpoint. It leads to stagnation, which ends in nothing.

Nothing is not the same as the deeps of space, despite all appearances to the contrary. Space is not a vacuum: it contains random localized events, myriad suns and stars, the possibility of planets that can support life. The deeps are chaotic and unfathomable, frightening in their unknowability, but they are rich, dripping with potential. Nothing is nothing, a barren waste, an eerily silent planet with no animals, no birds, just water and dirt, the absence of free will and the chaos that free will brings with it. The deeps are best represented by the planet from the beginning of *Prometheus*: rocky mountains and rushing waters and abundant plant life: fertile terrain waiting for created beings to walk on it. The Engineer planet from *Alien: Covenant* represents nothing: cypress trees waving in the wind, a necropolis filled with fossilized bodies, a silent planet after the end of the lives it once sustained, hospitable only to the aliens who visit death on anyone who lands in their territory.

Evil in *Alien: Covenant* is the same as it was in *Prometheus*, and in *Alien: Resurrection*, and in all the other *Alien* films before them. It is the attempt to assert control over chaos, to repurpose what has already been created through exploitation, and in so doing, destroying it. It is a denial of the potential of all that is yet to come, present and future, and it is the use of that potential for personal gain. It is the discreation of others, the negation of their personhood and the denial of their inherent worth.

EPILOGUE

The *Alien* series and Catherine Keller's *Face of the Deep* resonate on the same frequency. Both concern themselves with challenging previously established and accepted norms—Keller, with creation *ex nihilo*, and *Alien*, with readings of science fiction and horror as pulpy genre exercises. Readings of each one inform the other. Keller's *Face of the Deep*, by necessity complex, is easier to swallow when considered through the lens of cosmic horror stories like *Alien*. The *Alien* series, in turn, makes more sense as a whole when viewed with Keller's cosmology and understanding of evil in mind.

Both texts demonstrate evil as attempts to control the uncontrollable, which by necessity flatten complexity into homogeneity, drawing hard boundaries around complexity until freedom is destroyed. For *Alien*, cycles of use and discreation must be fought tooth and nail, whether the discreation comes in the form of the alien itself or in the form of exploitative Companies and worldviews. For Keller, to exist in the world is to live on the edge of chaos, and where living ethically demands that "the flowing potentiality of each actuality, each creature, realizes itself in limitation."[1] For both, evil is not violence, nor is it the void of the unknown. Instead, it is the act of exploitation, which might take place as acts of violence, but which

1. Keller, *Face of the Deep*, 7.   113

solidifies into patterns and cycles of denying the freedoms and personhood of others.

BIBLIOGRAPHY

Anderson, Cheryl B. *Ancient Laws and Contemporary Controversies: The Need for Inclusive Biblical Interpretation*. Oxford: Oxford University Press, 2009.

Asimov, Isaac. *I, Robot*. New York: Doubleday, 1950.

Baker-Fletcher, Karen. *Dancing with God: The Trinity from a Womanist Perspective*. St. Louis: Chalice, 2006.

Baumann, Rebecca, and Jody Mitchell. "Artificial Life." In *Frankenstein 200: The Birth, Life, and Resurrection of Mary Shelley's Monster*, 116–21. Bloomington, IN: Indiana University Press, 2018.

Bogost, Ian. *Alien Phenomenology, or What It's Like to Be a Thing*. Minneapolis: University of Minnesota Press, 2012.

Boon, Kevin Alexander. "Episteme-Ology of Science Fiction." *Journal of the Fantastic in the Arts* 11 (2001) 359–74.

Busch, Eberhard. *The Great Passion: An Introduction to Karl Barth's Theology*. Translated by Geoffrey W. Bromily. Edited by Judith and Darrell Guder. Grand Rapids: Eerdmans, 2004.

Byars, Jackie, et al. "Symposium on 'Alien' (Un Symposium Sur 'Alien')." *Science Fiction Studies* 7 (1980) 278–304.

Caeners, Torsten. "Negotiating the Human in Ridley Scott's *Prometheus*." In *Posthumanism in Young Adult Fiction: Finding Humanity in a Posthuman World*, edited by Anita Tarr and Donna R. White, 199–226. Jackson: University Press of Mississippi, 2018.

Cameron, James, dir. *Aliens*. 1986; Beverly Hills, Twentieth Century Fox: Twentieth Century Fox Home Entertainment, 2014. DVD.

Carpenter, Ginette. "Mothers and Others." In *Women and the Gothic: An Edinburgh Companion*, edited by Avril Horner and Sue Zlosnik, 46–59. Edinburgh: Edinburgh University Press, 2016.

Cobbs, John L. "'Alien' as an Abortion Parable." In *Literature/Film Quarterly* 18 (1990) 198–201.

Collins, Michael J. "The Body of the Work of the Body: Physio-Textuality in Contemporary Horror." In *Journal of the Fantastic in the Arts* 5 (1993) 28–35.

Copier, Laura. "Maternal Martyrdom: Alien3 and the Power of the Female Martyr." In *Powers: Religion as a Social and Spiritual Force*, edited by Meerten B. Ter Borg and Jan Willem Van Henten, 275–92. New York: Fordham University Press, 2010.

Creed, Barbara. *The Monstrous-Feminine: Film, Feminism, Psychoanalysis*. New York: Routledge, 1993.

Csicsery-Ronay, Istvan. "On the Grotesque in Science Fiction." In *Science Fiction Studies* 29 (2002) 71–99.

de Lauzirika, Charles, dir. *The Beast Within: The Making of Alien*. 2003; Beverly Hills, Twentieth Century Fox: Twentieth Century Fox Home Entertainment, 2003. DVD.

Doane, Mary Ann. "Technophilia: Technology, Representation, and the Feminine." In *Liquid Metal: The Science Fiction Film Reader*, edited by Sean Redmond, 182–90. New York: Columbia University Press, 2007.

Dorrien, Gary. "Dialectics of Difference: Barth, Whitehead, Modern Theology and the Uses of Worldviews." In *American Journal of Theology and Philosophy* 30 (2009) 244–70.

Doyle, Sady. *Dead Blondes and Bad Mothers*. New York: Penguin Random House, 2019.

Dreyer, Carl Theodor. *The Passion of Joan of Arc*. 1928; Paris, Société générale des films: The Criterion Collection, 2018. Blu-Ray.

Ebert, Roger. *Sneak Previews*. "Take 2: Invasion of the Outer Space Movies." Hosted by Gene Siskel and Roger Ebert. Chicago: WTTW National Productions, 1980.

Fincher, David, dir. *Alien 3*. 1992; Beverly Hills, Twentieth Century Fox: Twentieth Century Fox Home Entertainment, 2014. DVD.

Flanagan, Martin. "The Alien Series and Generic Hybridity." In *Alien Identities: Exploring Differences in Film and Fiction*, edited by Deborah Cartmell et al., 156–71. London: Pluto, 1999.

Frakes, Randall, et al. *James Cameron's Story of Science Fiction*. Los Angeles: Insight Editions, 2018.

Gallardo C., Ximena, and C. Jason Smith. *Alien Woman: The Making of Lt. Ellen Ripley*. London: Continuum, 2004.

Grant, Barry Keith. "Sensuous Elaboration: Reason and the Visible in the Science Fiction Film." In *Liquid Metal: The Science Fiction Film Reader*, edited by Sean Redmond, 17–23. New York: Columbia University Press, 2007.

Haraway, Donna J. "A Manifesto for Cyborgs: Science, Technology and Socialist Feminism in the 1980s." In *Liquid Metal: The Science Fiction Film Reader,* edited by Sean Redmond, 158–81. New York: Columbia University Press, 2007.

Hart, John. "Xenophilia and Xenophobia: Good Alien or Evil Alien from Space?" In *Encountering ETI: Aliens in Avatar and the Americas,* 134–66. London: Lutterworth, 2014.

Hurley, Kelly. "Reading Like an Alien: Posthuman Identity in Ridley Scott's *Alien* and David Cronenberg's *Rabid.*" In *Posthuman Bodies,* 203–24. Bloomington, IN: Indiana University Press, 1995.

Janca-Aji, Joyce. "The Dark Dreamlife of Postmodern Theology: *Delicatessen, The City of Lost Children,* and *Alien Resurrection.*" In *Religion and Science Fiction,* edited by James F. McGrath, 9–31. London: Lutterworth, 2011.

Jeunet, Jean-Pierre, dir. *Alien: Resurrection.* 1997; Beverly Hills, Twentieth Century Fox: Twentieth Century Fox Home Entertainment, 2014. DVD.

Johnson, Brian. "Prehistories of Posthumanism: Cosmic Indifferentism, Alien Genesis, and Ecology from H. P. Lovecraft to Ridley Scott." In *The Age of Lovecraft,* edited by Carl H. Sederholm, 97–116. Minneapolis: University of Minnesota Press, 2016.

Keegan, Rebecca. *The Futurist: the Life and Films of James Cameron.* New York: Crown, 2009.

Keller, Catherine. *Face of the Deep: A Theology of Becoming.* London: Routledge, 2003.

Kristeva, Julia. *Powers of Horror: An Essay On Abjection.* New York: Columbia University Press, 1982.

Lean, David. *Lawrence of Arabia.* 1962; Culver City: Columbia Tristar Home Entertainment, 2003. DVD.

Lev, Peter. "Whose Future? 'Star Wars,' 'Alien,' and 'Blade Runner.'" *Literature/Film Quarterly* 26 (1998) 30–37.

Linton, Patricia. "Aliens, (M)Others, Cyborgs." In *Alien Identities: Exploring Differences in Film and Fiction,* edited by Deborah Cartmell, 172–86. London: Pluto, 1999.

LoBrutto, Vincent. *Ridley Scott: A Biography.* Lexington: University Press of Kentucky, 2019.

Malmgren, Carl D. "Self and Other in SF: Alien Encounters." *Science Fiction Studies* 20 (1993) 15–33.

McDowell, John C. "Much Ado About Nothing: Karl Barth's Being Unable to Do Nothing about Nothingness." *International Journal of Systematic Theology* 4 (2002) 319–35.

McGrath, James F. *Theology and Science Fiction*. Eugene, OR: Cascade, 2016.

McIntee, David. *Beautiful Monsters: The Unofficial and Unauthorised Guide to the Alien and Predator Films*. Canterbury: Telos, 2005.

Melzer, Patricia. "Technoscience's Stepdaughter: The Feminist Cyborg in Alien Resurrection." In *Alien Constructions: Science Fiction and Feminist Thought*, 108–48. Austin: University of Texas Press, 2006.

Monk, Patricia. *Alien Theory: The Alien As Archetype in the Science Fiction Short Story*. Lanham: Scarecrow, 2006.

Neale, Steve. "You've Got To Be Fucking Kidding! Knowledge, Belief, and Judgment in Science Fiction." In *Liquid Metal: The Science Fiction Film Reader*, edited by Sean Redmond, 11–16. New York: Columbia University Press, 2007.

Peters, Ted. "The Implications of the Discovery of Extra-Terrestrial Life for Religion." *Philosophical Transactions: Mathematical, Physical and Engineering Sciences*, 369 (2011) 644–55.

Philippe, Alexandre O, dir. *Memory: The Origins of Alien*. 2019; Denver: Exhibit A Pictures, 2019.

Philnus, Robert M. *Visions and Re-Visions: [Re]constructing Science Fiction*. Liverpool: Liverpool University Press, 2005.

Povich, Frank, dir. *Jodorowsky's Dune*. 2014; New York: Sony Pictures Classics, 2014. DVD.

Rinzler, J. W. *The Making of Alien*. London: Titan, 2019.

Salisbury, Mark. *Prometheus: The Art of the Film*. London: Titan, 2012.

Scanlon, Paul, and Michael Gross. *The Book of Alien*. London: Titan, 1993.

Schulweis, Harold M. "Karl Barth's Job: 'Morality and Theodicy.'" *The Jewish Quarterly Review* 65 (1975) 156–67.

Scobie, Stephen. "What's the Story, Mother?: The Mourning of the Alien." *Science Fiction Studies* 20 (1993) 80–93.

Scott, Ridley, dir. *Alien*. 1979; Beverly Hills, Twentieth Century Fox: Twentieth Century Fox Home Entertainment, 2014. DVD.

———. *Alien: Covenant*. 2017; Beverly Hills, Twentieth Century Fox: Twentieth Century Fox Home Entertainment, 2017. DVD.

———. *Prometheus*. 2012; Beverly Hills, Twentieth Century Fox: Twentieth Century Fox Home Entertainment, 2012. DVD.

Shelley, Mary Wollstonecraft. *Frankenstein, or The Modern Prometheus*. London: Puffin, 1994.

Shelley, Percy Bysshe. "Ozymandias." 1818. https://www. poetryfoundation.org/poems/46565/ozymandias.

Sobchack, Vivian. "Between a Rock and a Hard Place." *Film Comment* 48 (2012) 30–34.

Sölle, Dorothee, and Dianne L. Oliver. *Dorothee Soelle: Essential Writings*. Maryknoll: Orbis, 2006.

Suvin, Darko. *Metamorphoses of Science Fiction*. New Haven, CT: Yale University Press, 1979.

Stocker, Margarita. "God in Theory: Milton, Literature, and Theodicy." *Literature and Theology* 1 (1987) 70–88.

Taubes, Jacob. "Theodicy and Theology: A Philosophical Analysis of Karl Barth's Dialectical Theology." *The Journal of Religion* 34 (1954) 231–43.

Titan Books. *Alien: the Archive: the Ultimate Guide to the Classic Movies*. London: Titan, 2014.

Ward, Graham. "Barth and Postmodernism." *New Blackfriars* 74 (1993) 550–56.

Ward, Simon. *Aliens: the Set Photography: Behind the Scenes of James Cameron's 1986 Masterpiece*. London: Titan, 2016.

—————. *The Art and Making of* Alien: Covenant. London: Titan, 2017.

Warren, Calvin L. *Ontological Terror: Blackness, Nihilism, and Emancipation*. Durham, NC: Duke University Press, 2018.

Whittington, William (William Brian). *Sound Design and Science Fiction*. Austin: University of Texas Press, 2007.

Wolfe, Gary K. "Stasis and Chaos: Some Dynamics of Popular Genres." *Journal of the Fantastic in the Arts* 10 (1998) 4–16.

Yu, Anthony C. "Life in the Garden: Freedom and the Image of God in 'Paradise Lost': In Memoriam George Williamson." *The Journal of Religion* 60 (1980) 247–71.

Zoller Seitz, Matt (@mattzollerseitz). "30 Minutes on Alien." July 7, 2019. https://www.rogerebert.com/mzs/30-minutes-on-alien.

—————. "Alien: Covenant." May 15, 2017. https://www.rogerebert. com/reviews/alien-covenant-2017.

—————. "The original ALIEN was described by many critics, inaccurately, as haunted house movie in space, when it was actually a stalker film." May 5, 2017, 11:24 PM. Tweet. https:// twitter.com/mattzollerseitz/status/860711879408308230?s=20.

Printed in the USA
CPSIA information can be obtained
at www.ICGtesting.com
LVHW041535040524
779351LV00008B/534